Elemental Hawaiian Splendor

Photo Art of
Molly Hart and Kelly Hart

I0483251

Book and cover design by the authors

All photographs are by the authors

Paperback ISBN: 0-916289-42-7

Printed in the United States of America

First printing December, 2017

Hartworks LLC
P.O. Box 1984
Silver City, NM 88061

Email: theoffice@hartworks.com
Website: www.hartworks.com

Siblings Molly Hart and Kelly Hart have teamed up to present this book of their photographs taken in Hawaii. They chose to focus on the elemental power that is so prevalent in the islands. Hopefully these pages will convey the excitement and beauty of that wonderful place.

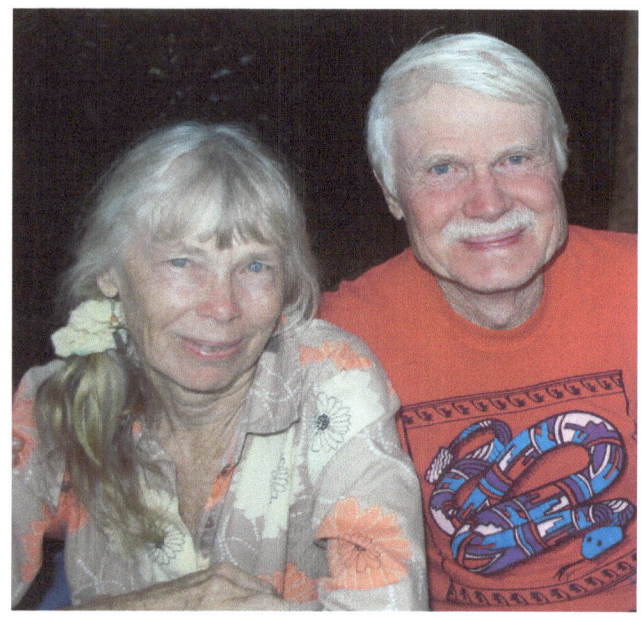

Molly Hart

Born into a family that encouraged multiple creative expressions, Kelly and I both picked up photography at an early age, and it has been a continuous thread in our lives ever since. An intersection came about when Kelly made his first trip to Hawaii in his 70's and was awed by the visceral visual landscape, thus germinating an idea to collaborate on a collection of images that spoke to the elemental spirit of Hawaii. I moved back to Hawaii in 2008, several decades after my first arrival in a home-built sailboat that our father helped to build in the mid 1960's. Early on I was drawn to the extraordinary clarity and saturation of the tropical light, and digital capturing of images allowed me a richer and more accessible expression.

Abundant subjects of sea, land and botanicals provide daily photo opportunities. My curiosity takes me deeper into an ordinary scene to find a more abstract expression that can take the viewer away from the original content into a more aesthetic experience of the inherent beauty. New technologies have given rise to the ability to create various interpretations of the raw data collected by the camera. Beyond the strictly documentary, the images create their own story, evoking a range of emotional responses. Love, respect, and aloha speak loudly throughout the story, from delicate tendrils to the awe inspiring power of the birth of new land.

Kelly Hart

Still photography has always been important to me, from my earliest Brownie camera as a child to my adoption of 35mm film as a teenager, and eventually engaging in the digital revolution. I had a darkroom in my closet when I was in high school and, once I started attending the University of California in Berkeley, I began a professional career as a photographer for several years. I took pictures for the Drama Department archives and did publicity stills for the Berkeley Folk Music Festival. Several of my photos graced the covers folk music albums, and I even managed to have several pages of my pictures appear in Playboy magazine chronicling a unique theatrical presentation with nude dancers on stage. After I left the University I attended the San Francisco Art Institute for awhile, studying photography and even used a large format view camera for some of the assignments. Soon after this my attention moved more toward cinematography and animation and for several decades I considered myself more of a filmmaker than a still photographer. I never gave up my still camera though, continuing to document my life and the surrounding world as the impulse came.

Several years ago I dug through my old negatives and slides from my days of living in the San Francisco Bay Area and decided to publish a book of these images titled *San Francisco's Psychedelic Sixties: A Photographic Trip with Kelly Hart*, now available at Amazon.com. I have an account at Flicker.com where you can view many of the pictures I've taken since I adopted digital imagery (see www.flickr.com/photos/kellyhart). It has been quite awhile since I have produced any films or video programs but I continue to thoroughly enjoy the process of taking still images as they emerge from my life. Creating this book with my sister Molly has been a marvelous opportunity to merge our inner visions of the vitality and splendor of all of the manifestations of life in Hawaii. I hope you enjoy the experience of viewing these images as much as we have enjoyed the process of creating them!

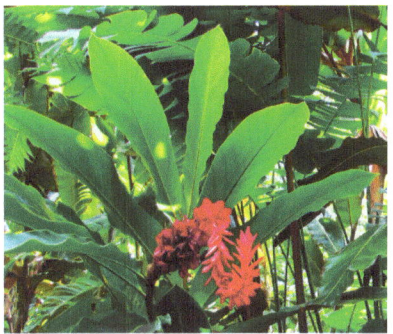

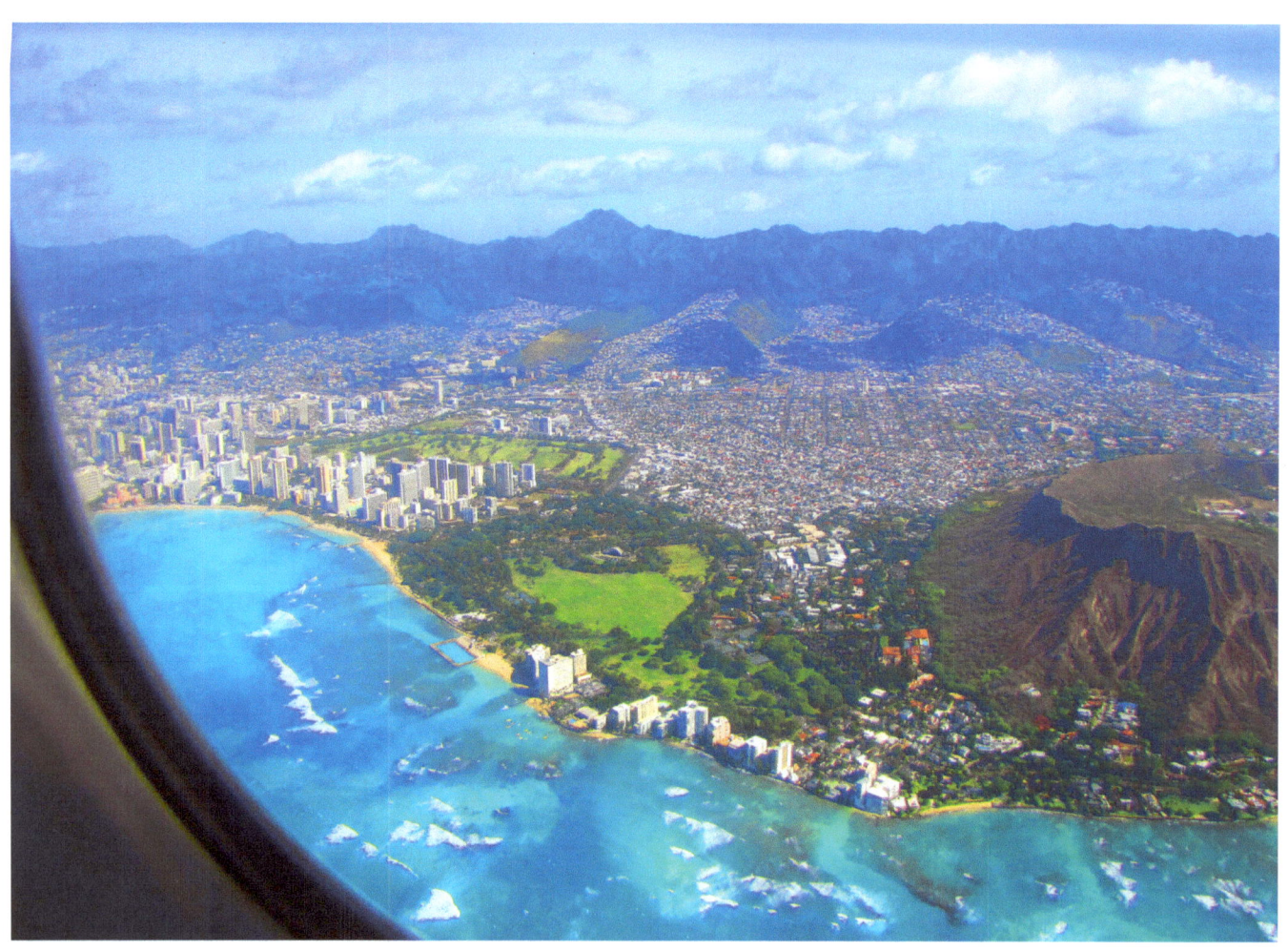

Approaching Honolulu   Kelly Hart

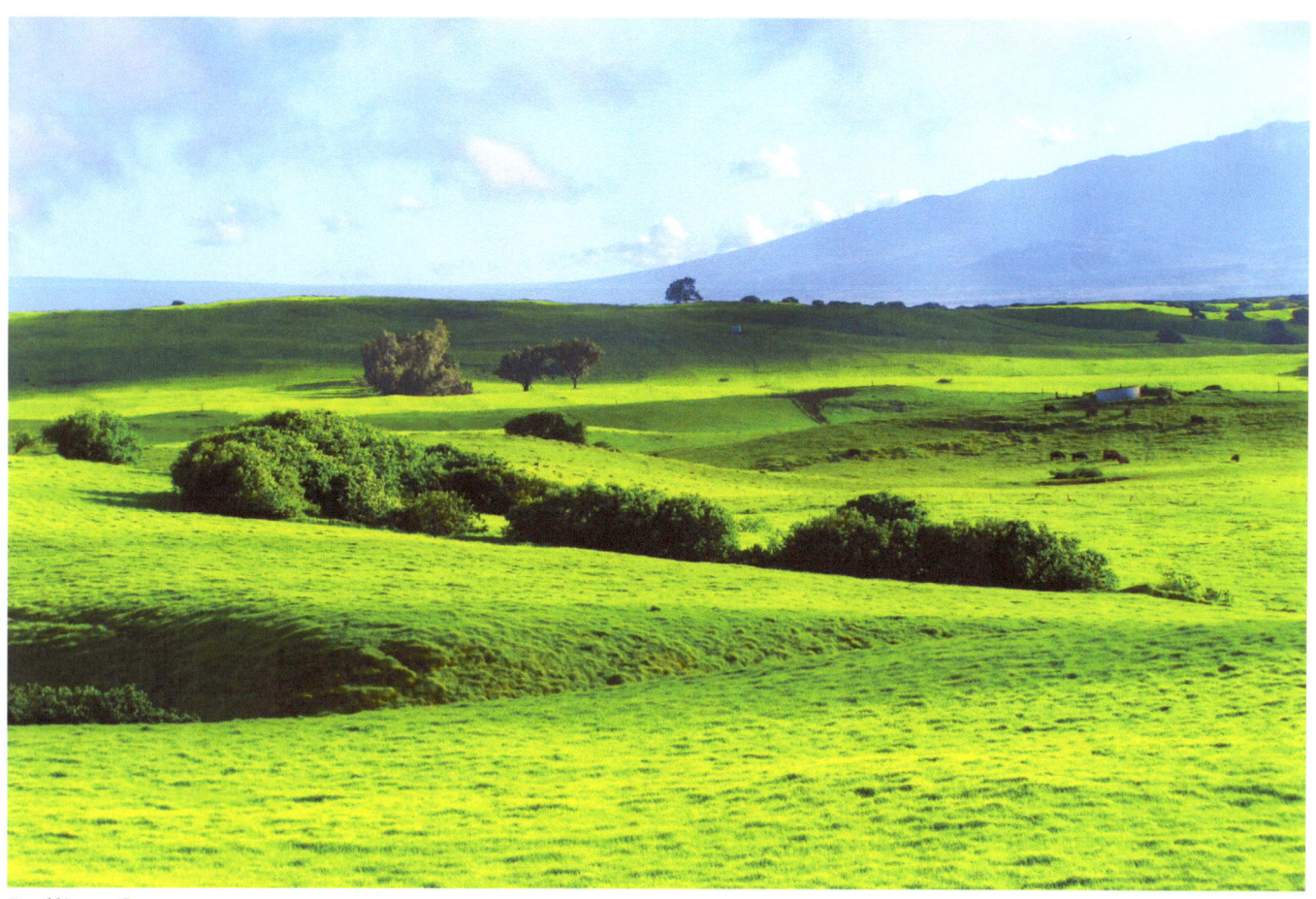

Rolling Country

Kelly Hart

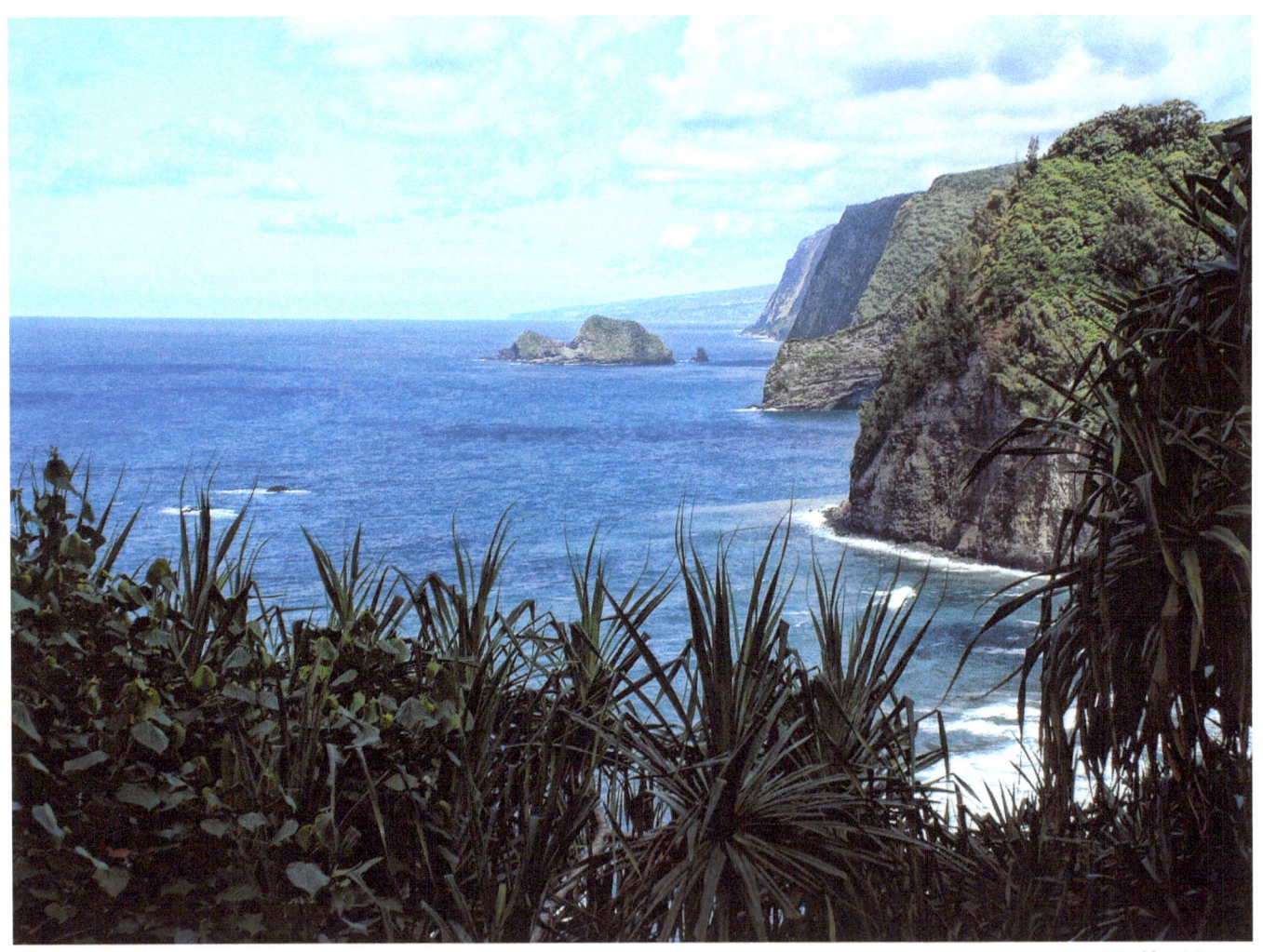

Pololu Valley

Molly Hart

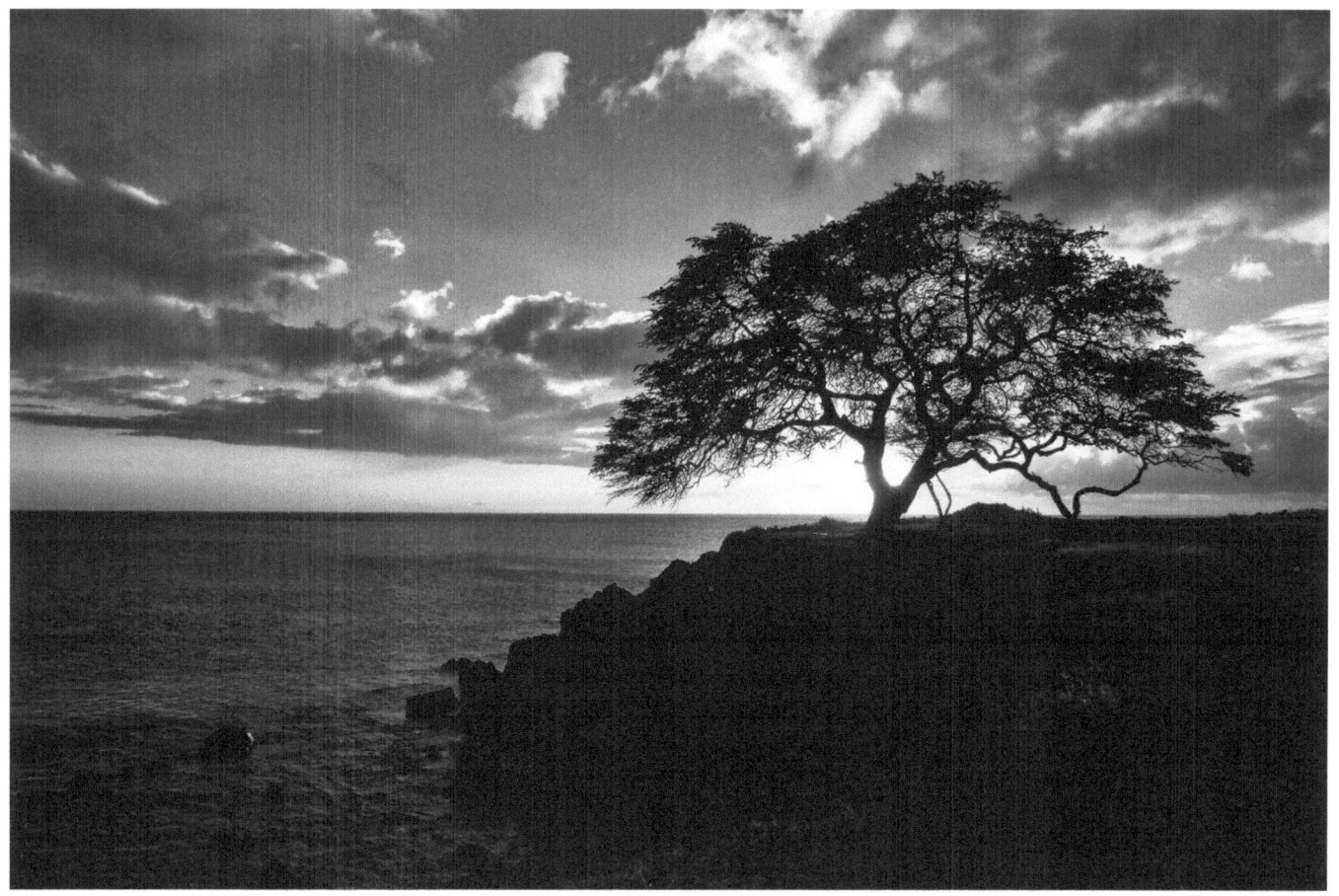

Kiawe Tree at Sunset   Molly Hart

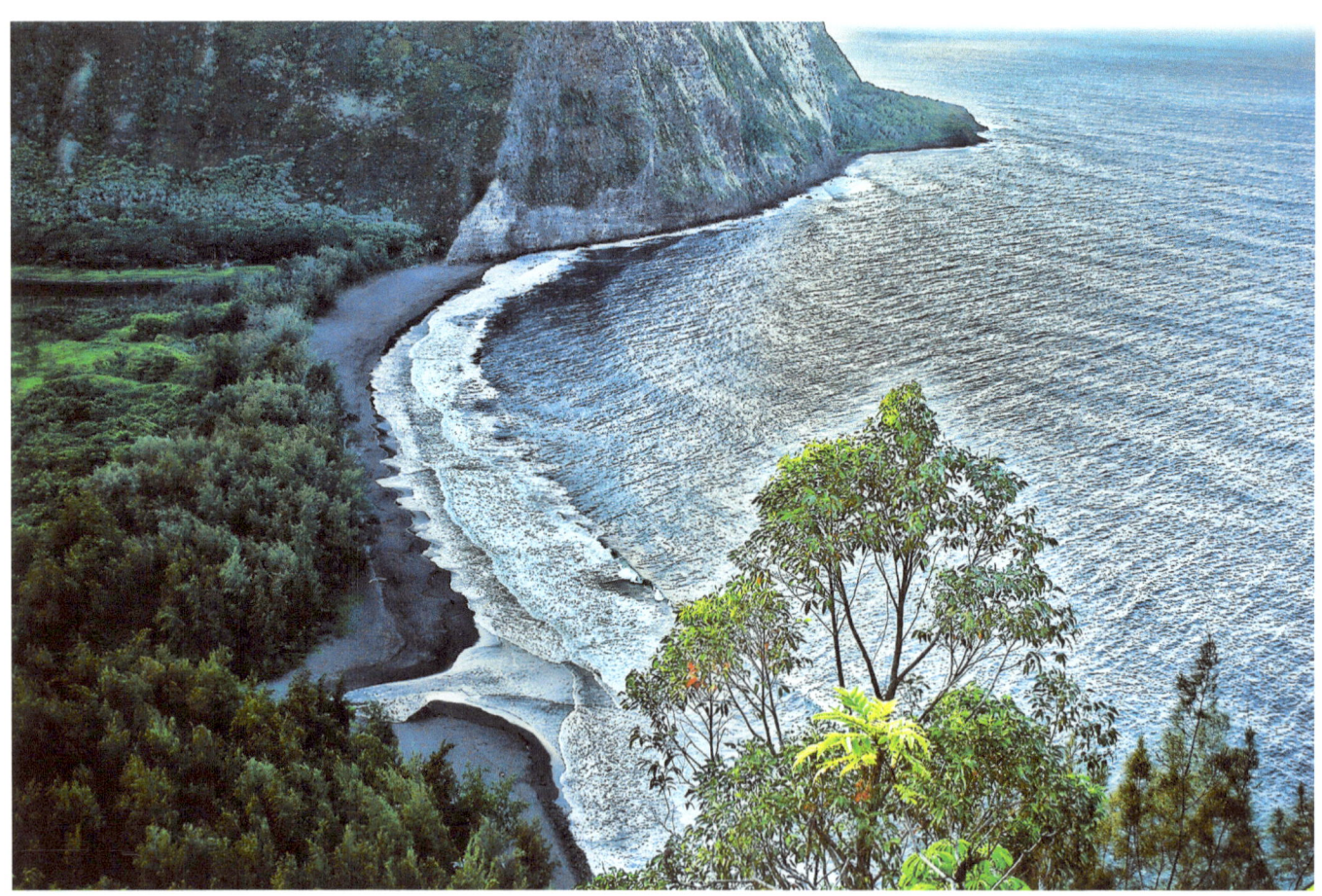

Waipio Valley   Molly Hart

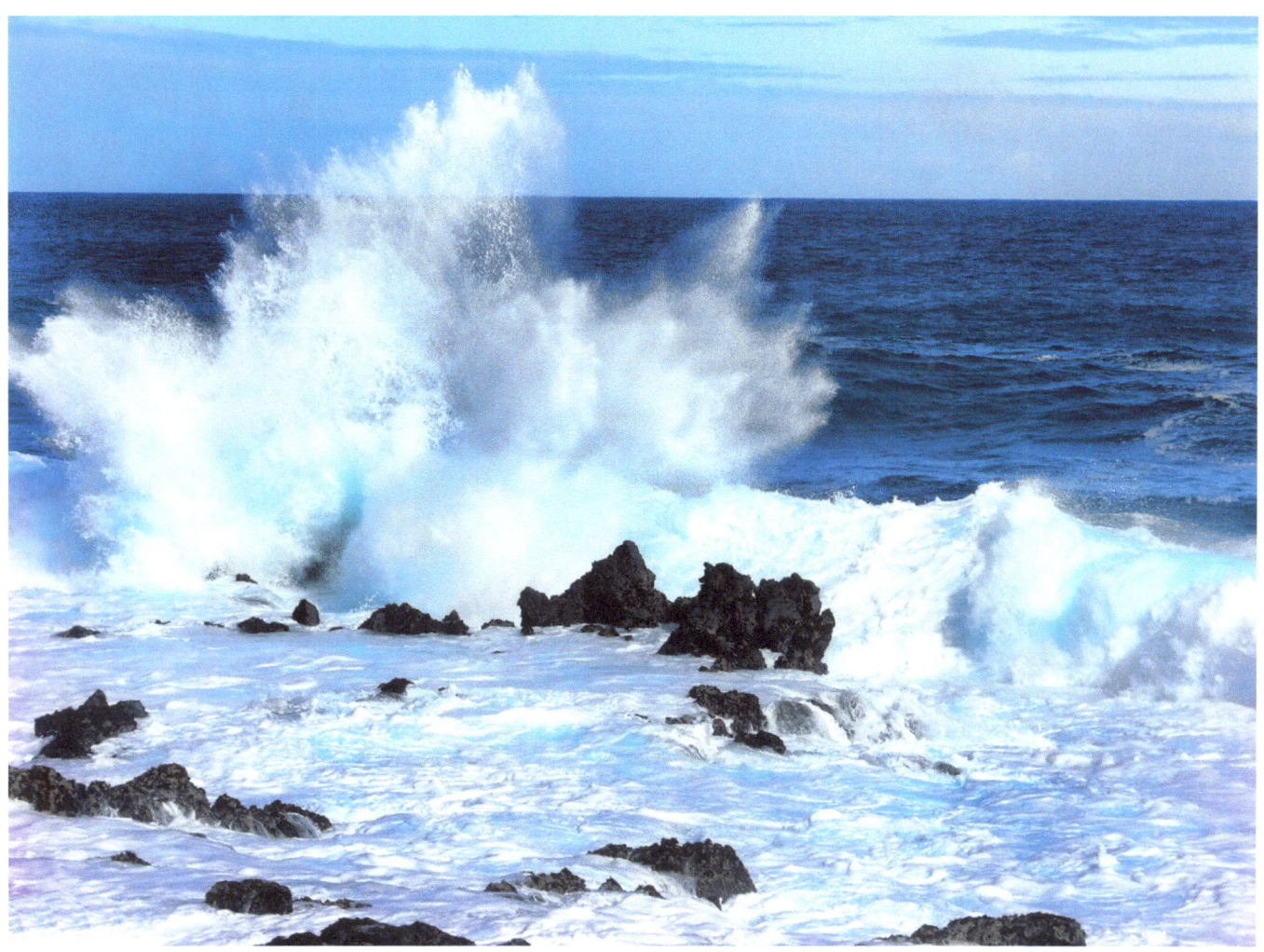

Laupāhoehoe Surf   Molly Hart

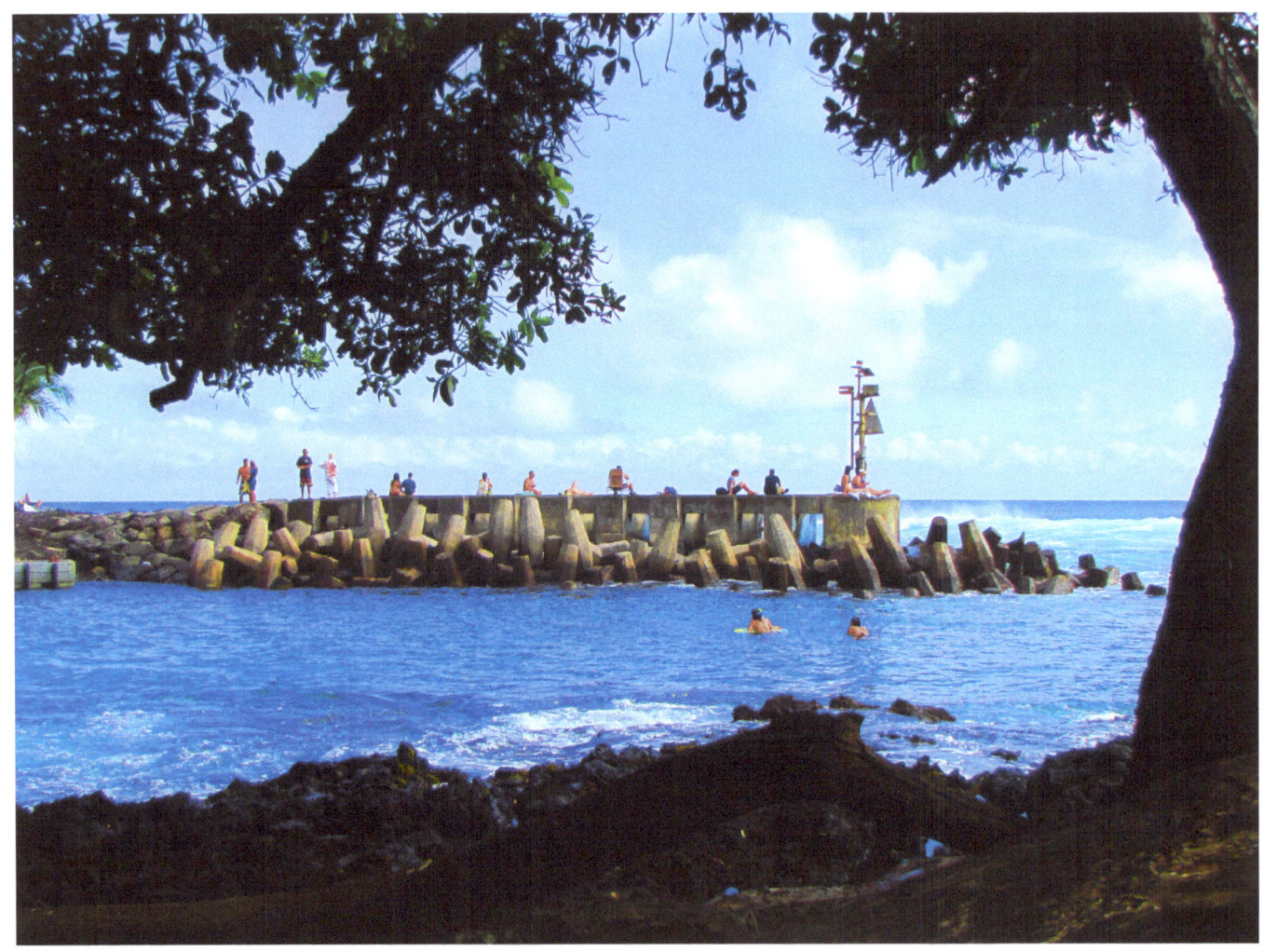

Pohoiki Pier

Kelly Hart

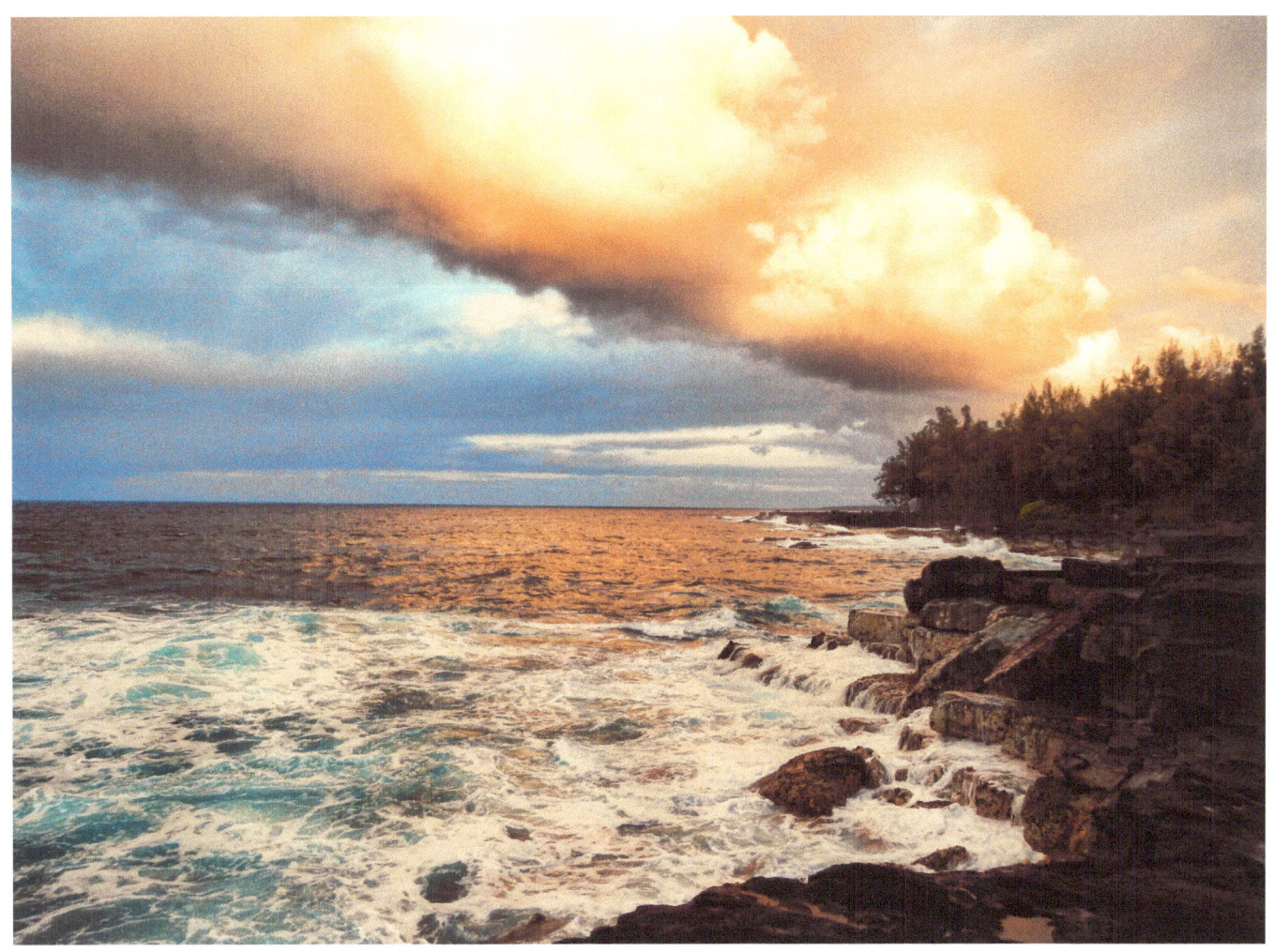

Maku'u Sunset   Molly Hart

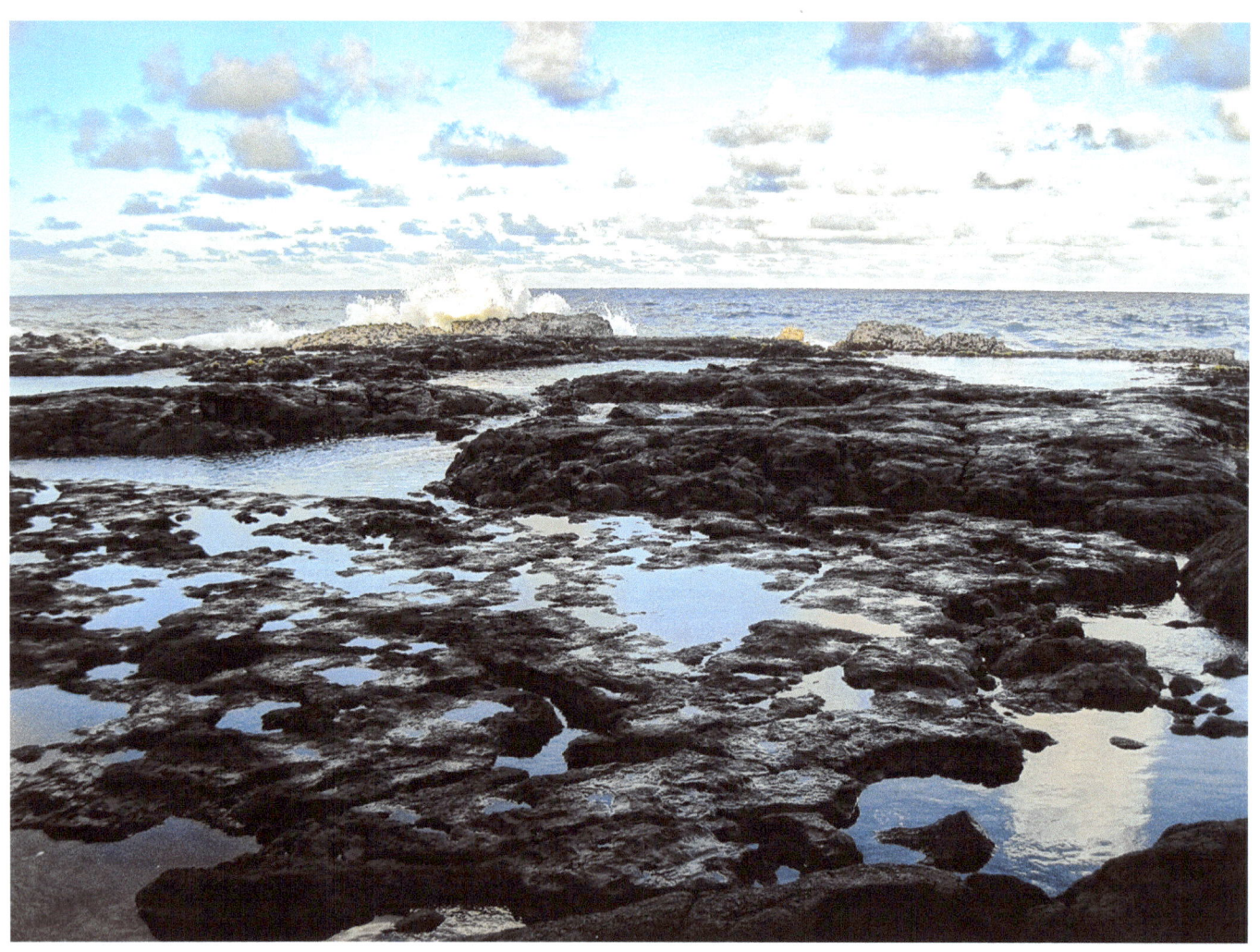

Tidepools

Molly Hart

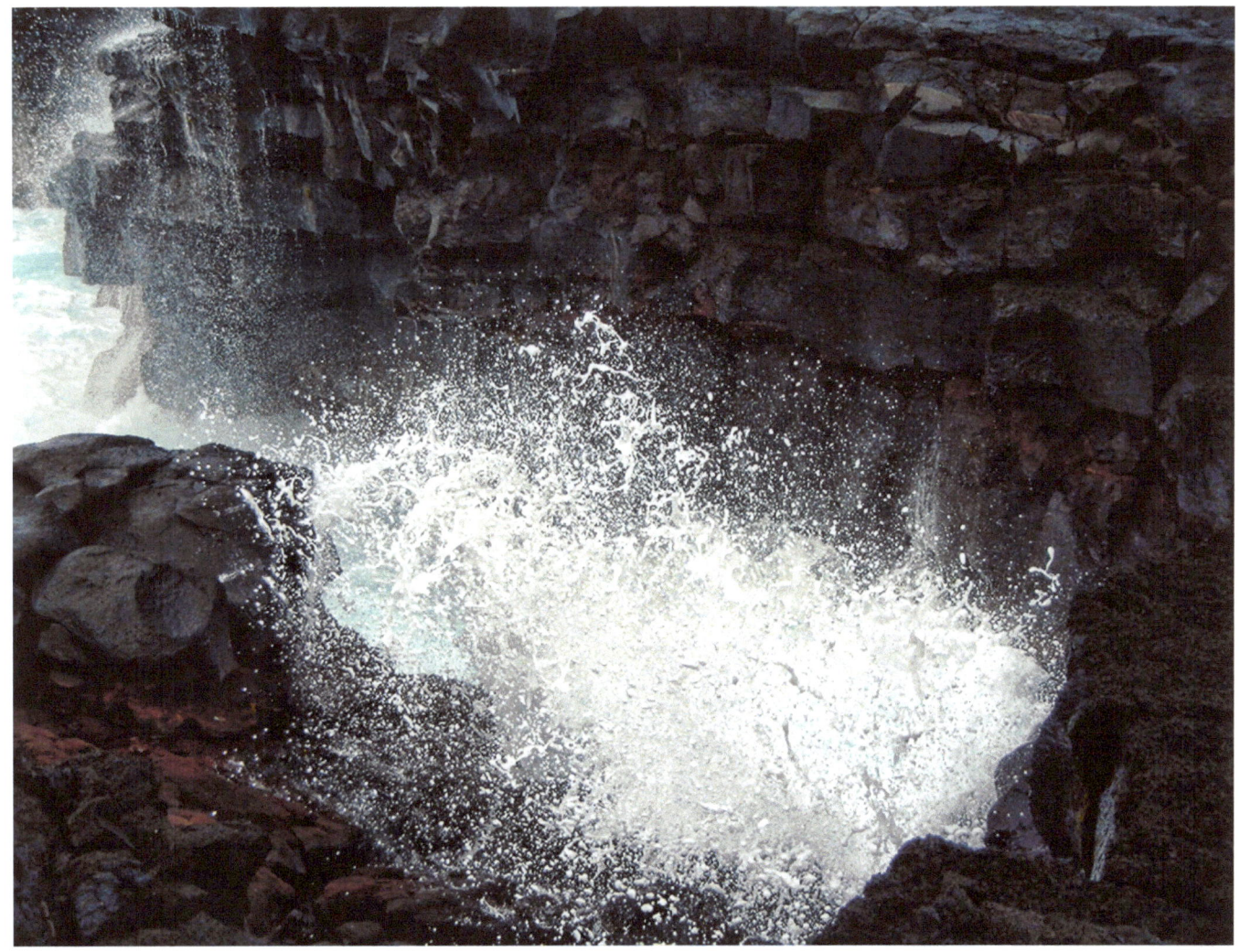

Blow Hole   Molly Hart

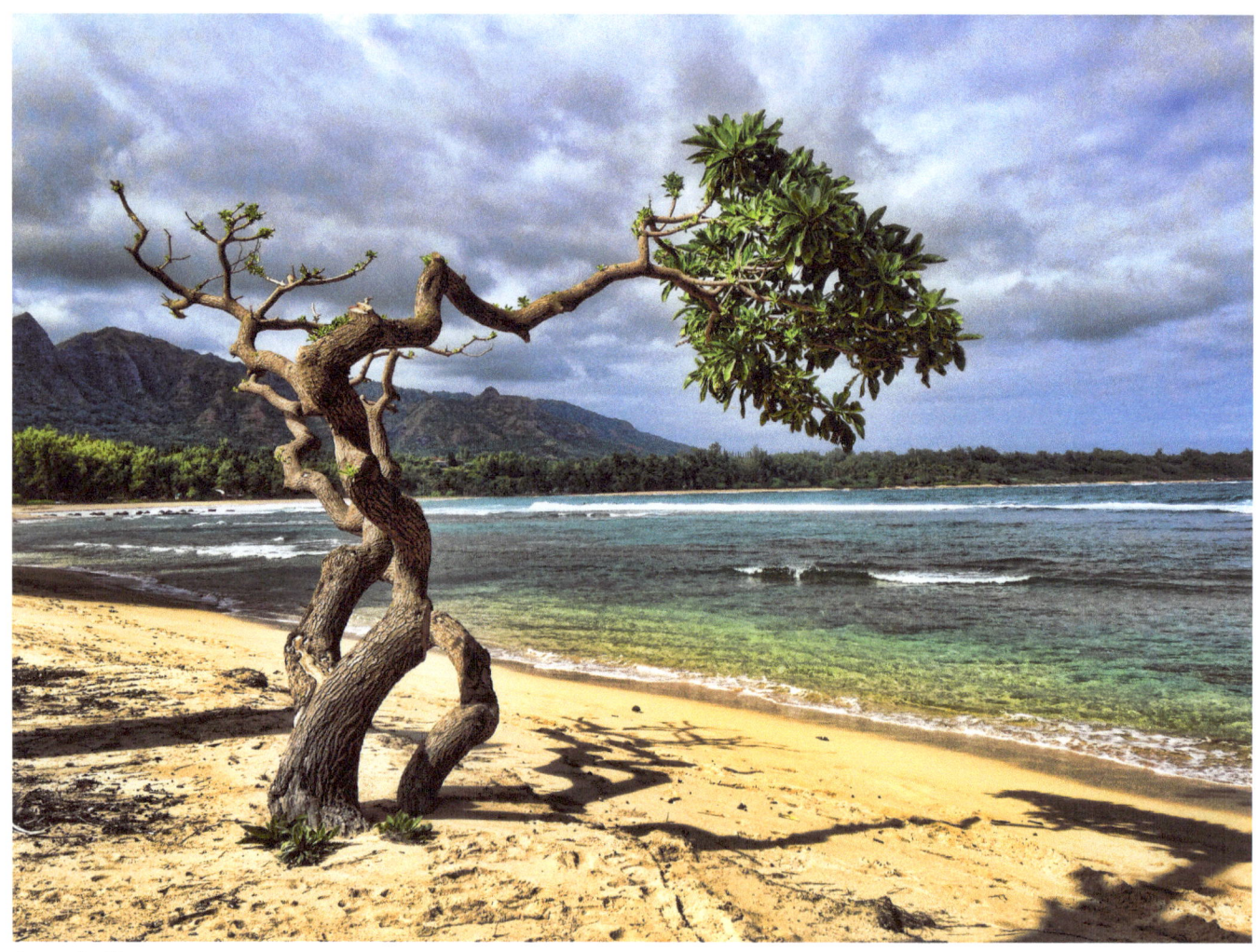

Beach Tree

Molly Hart

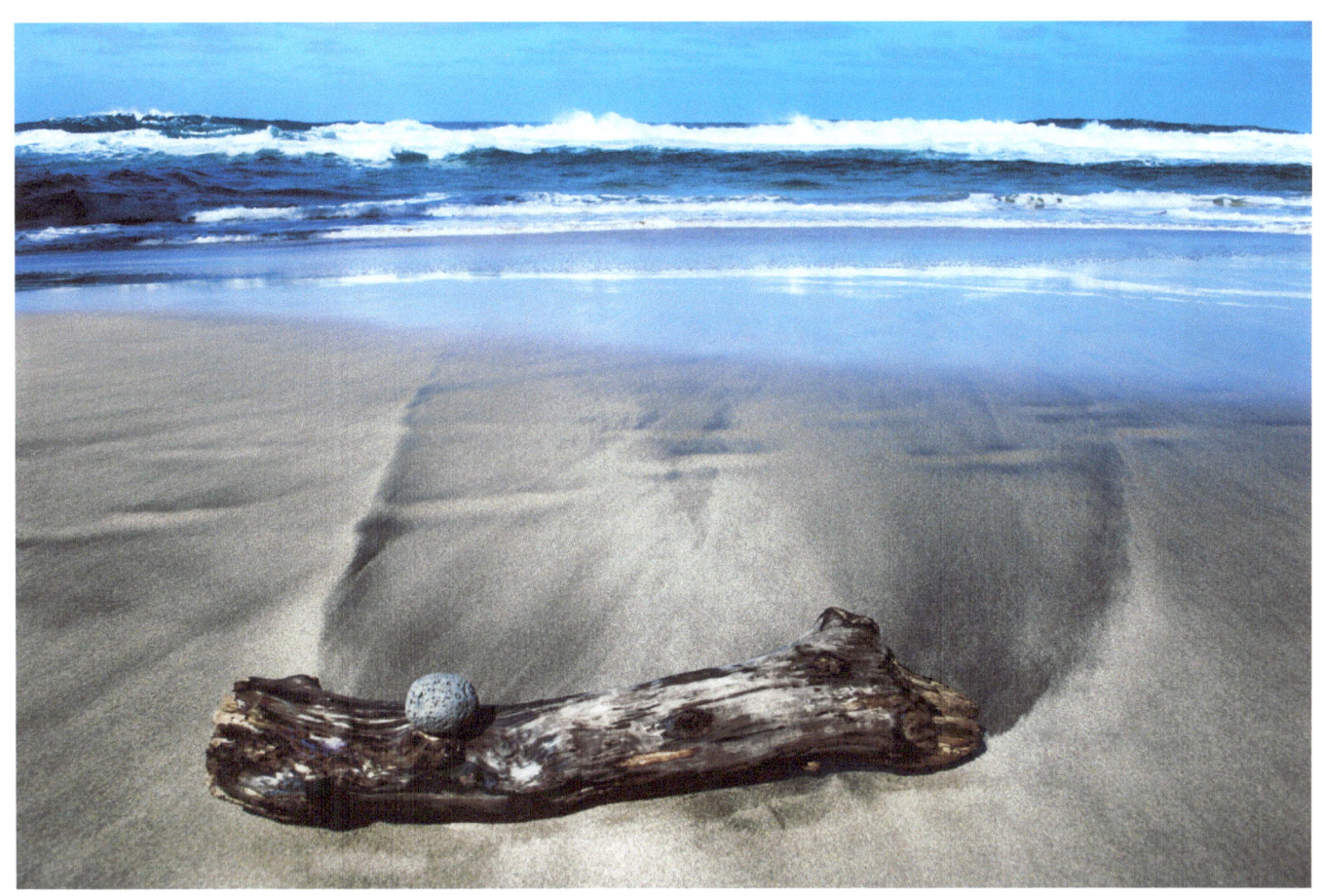

Driftwood

Molly Hart

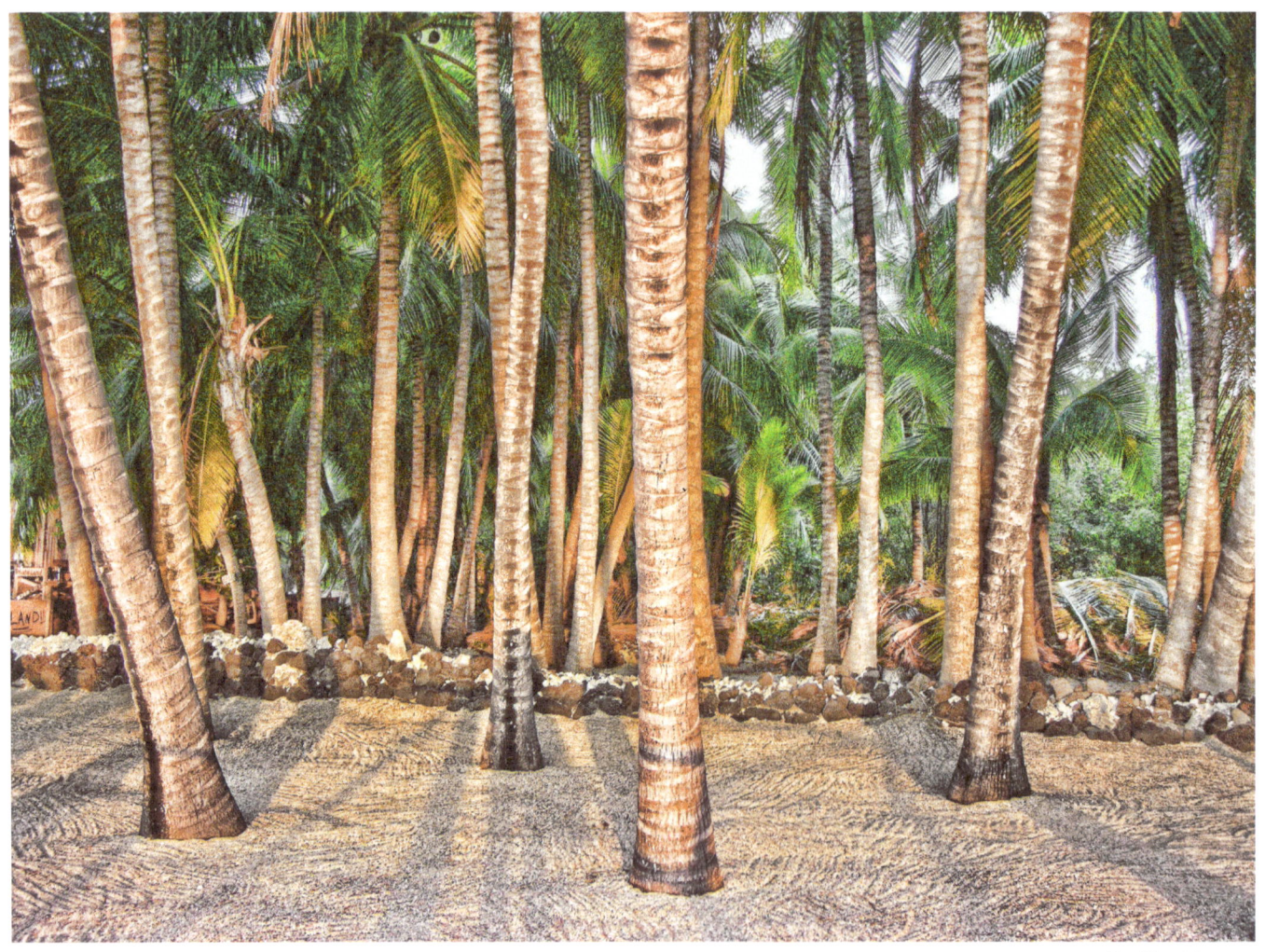

Cocos

Molly Hart

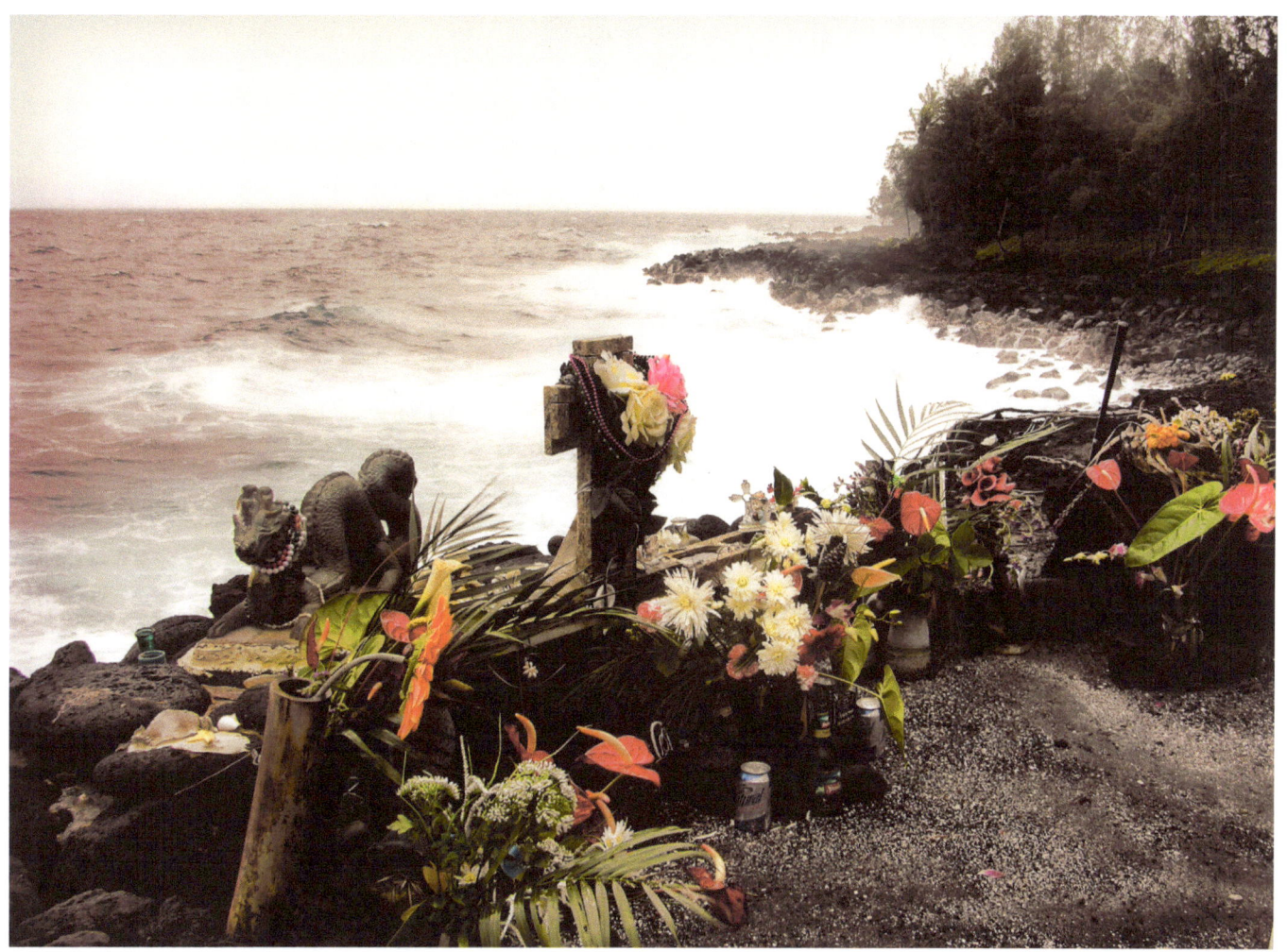

Homage

Molly Hart

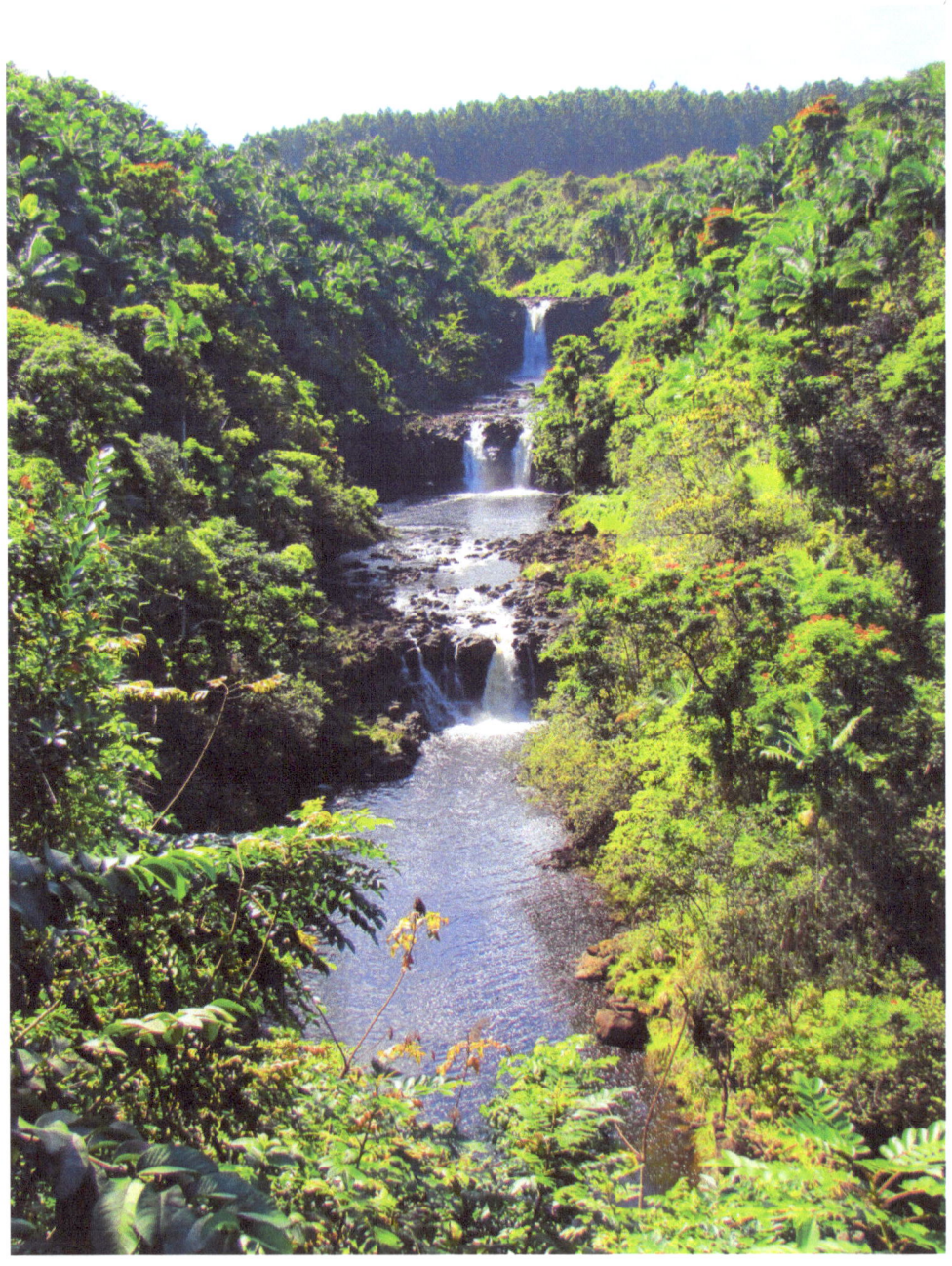

Umauma Falls   Kelly Hart

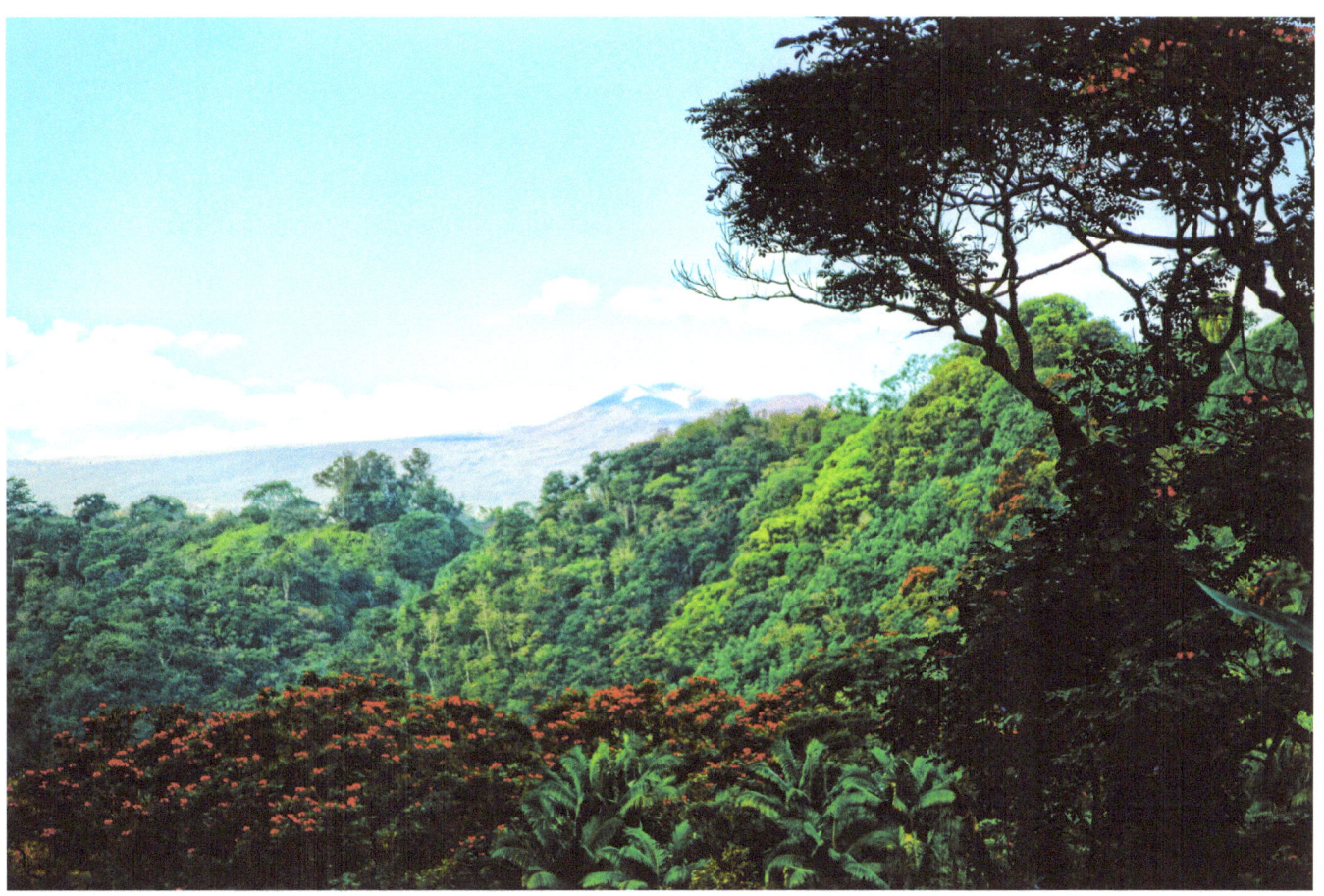

Mauna Kea Snow   Molly Hart

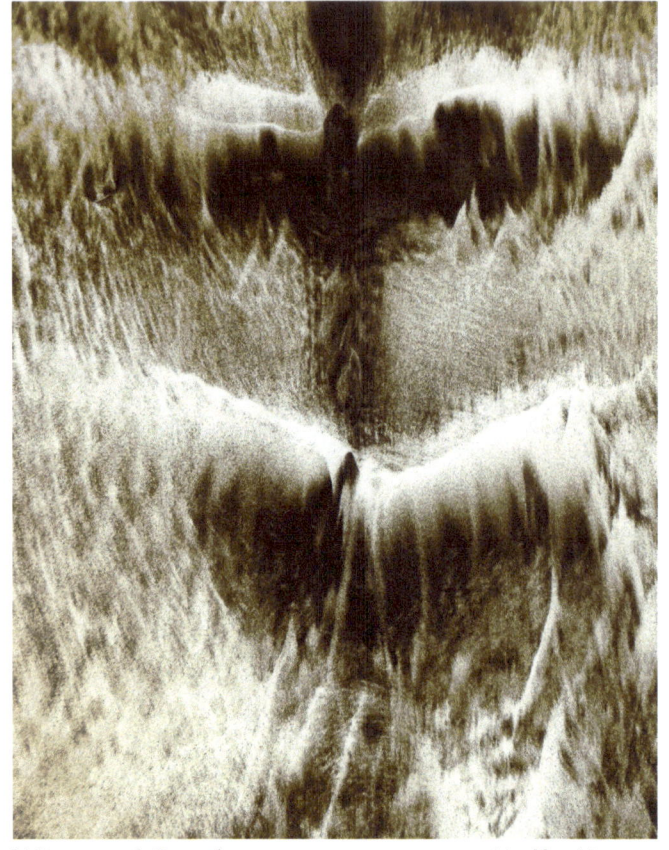

Wings of Sand   Molly Hart

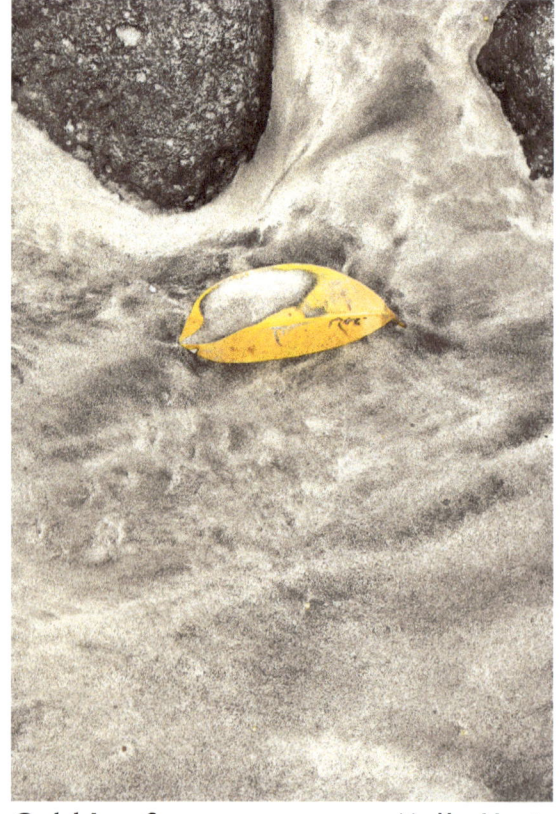

Gold Leaf   Molly Hart

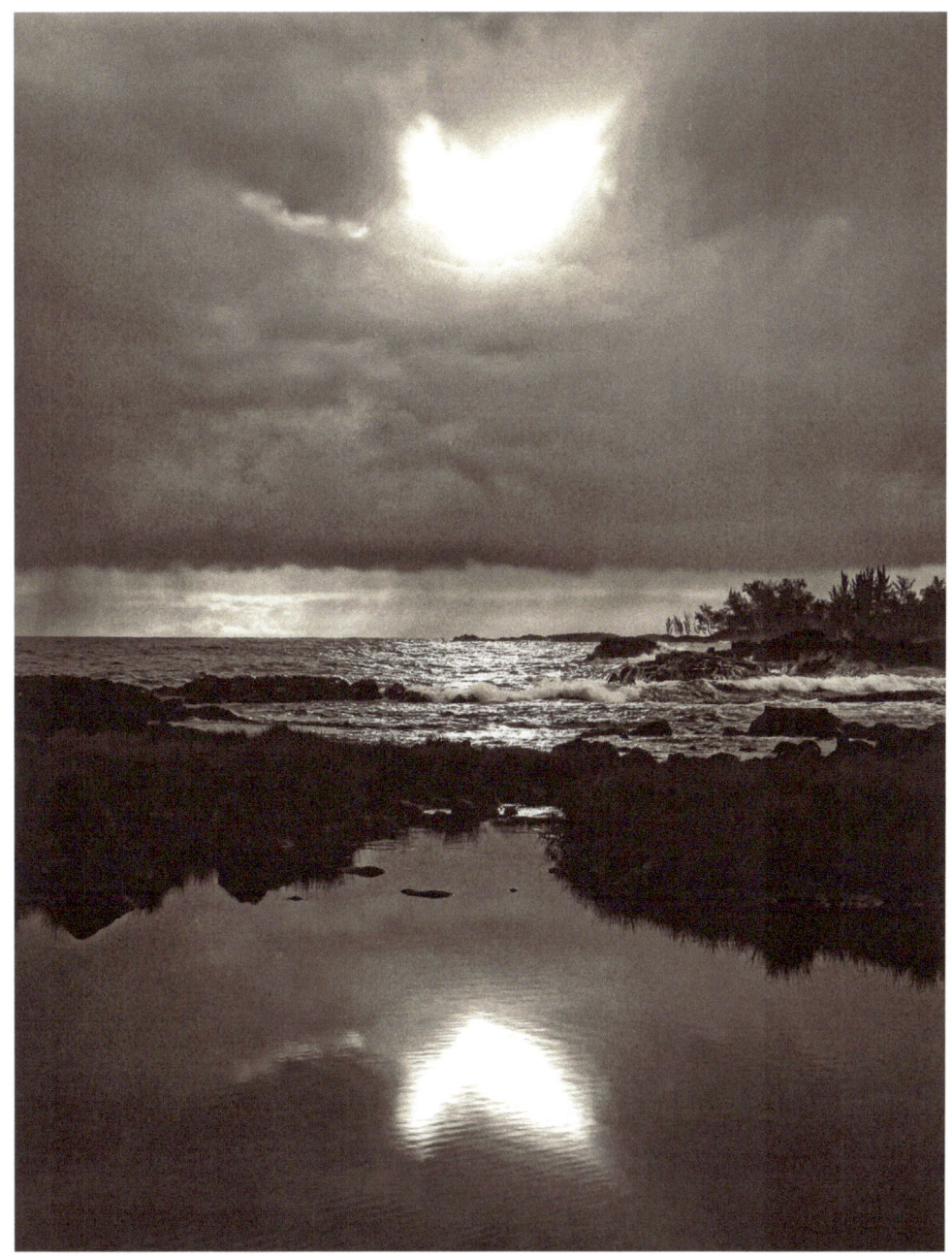

The Heart of Dawn   Molly Hart

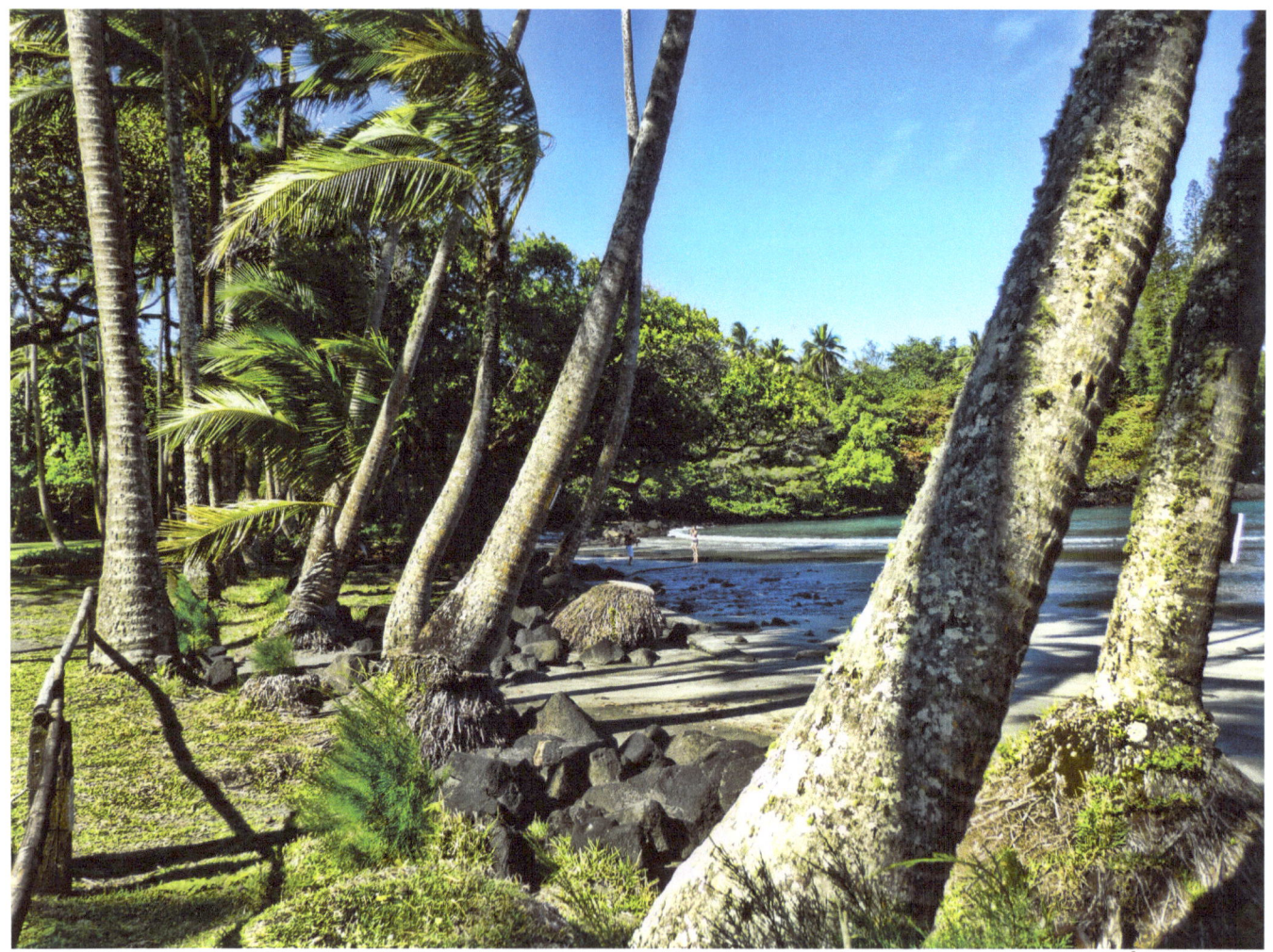

Ha'ena Beach   Molly Hart

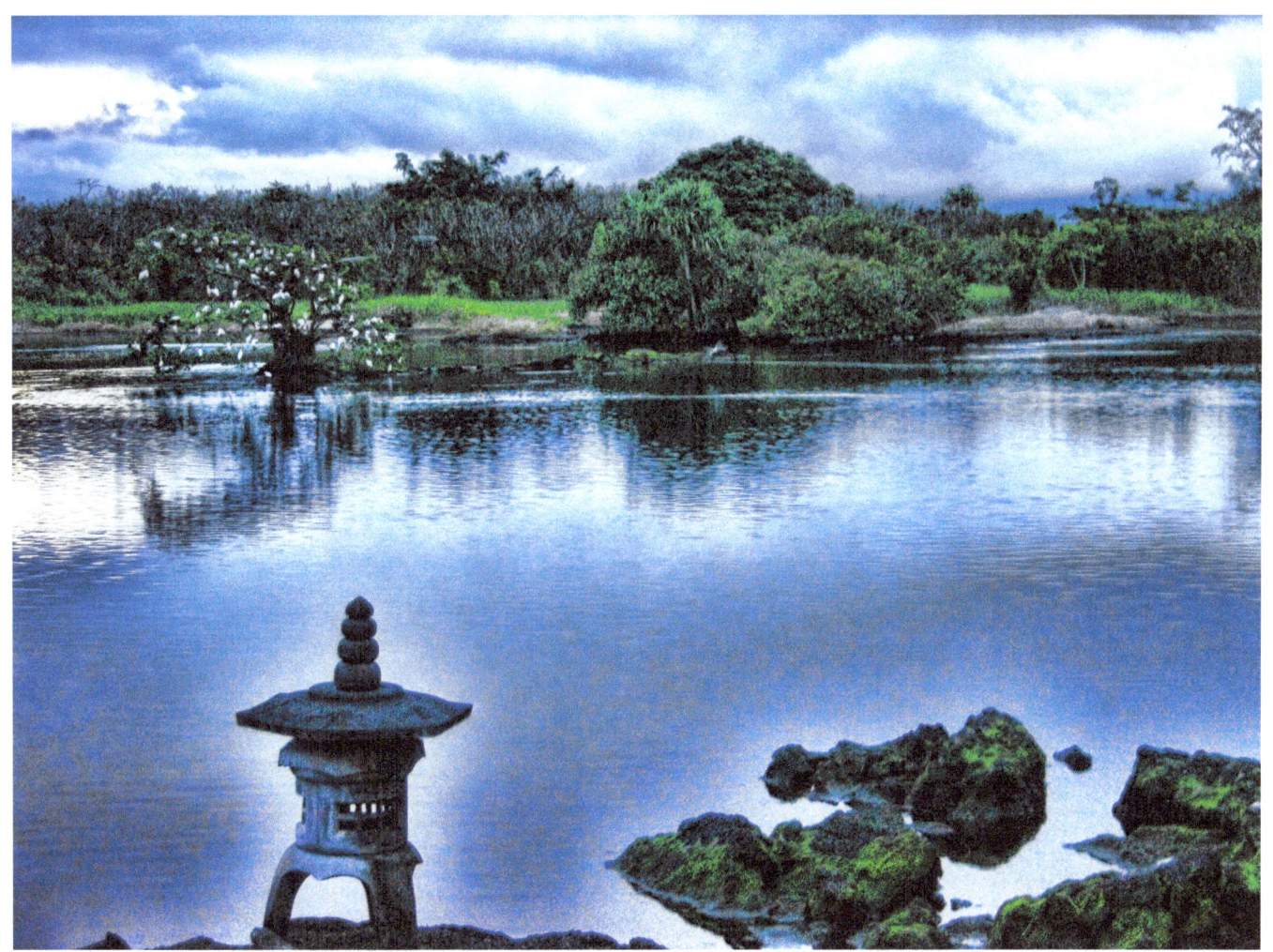

Egrets Roosting   Molly Hart

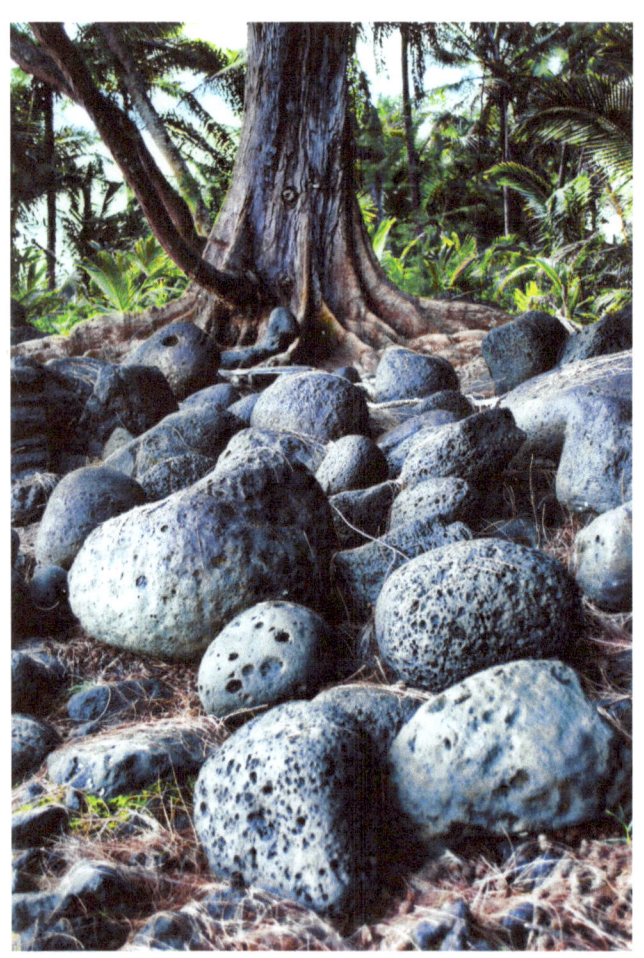

Sea Boulders   Molly Hart

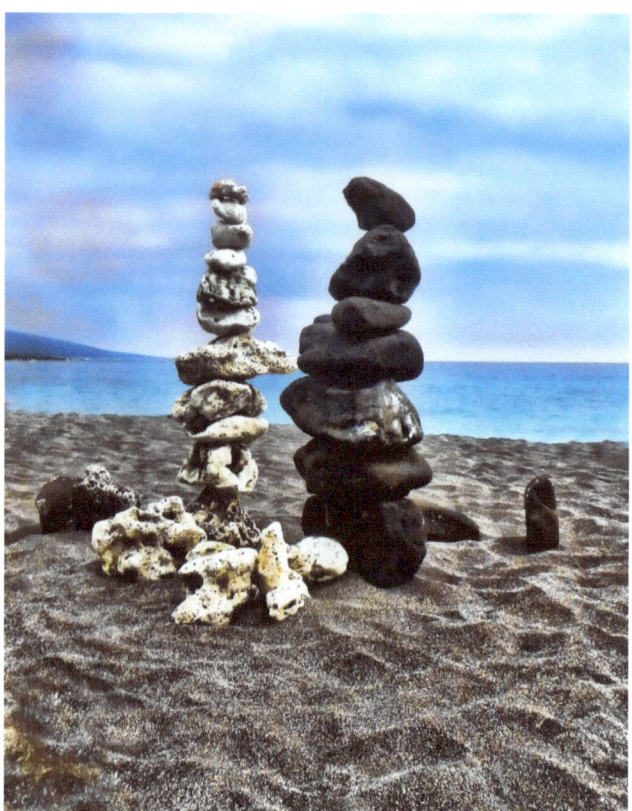

Lava & Coral   Molly Hart

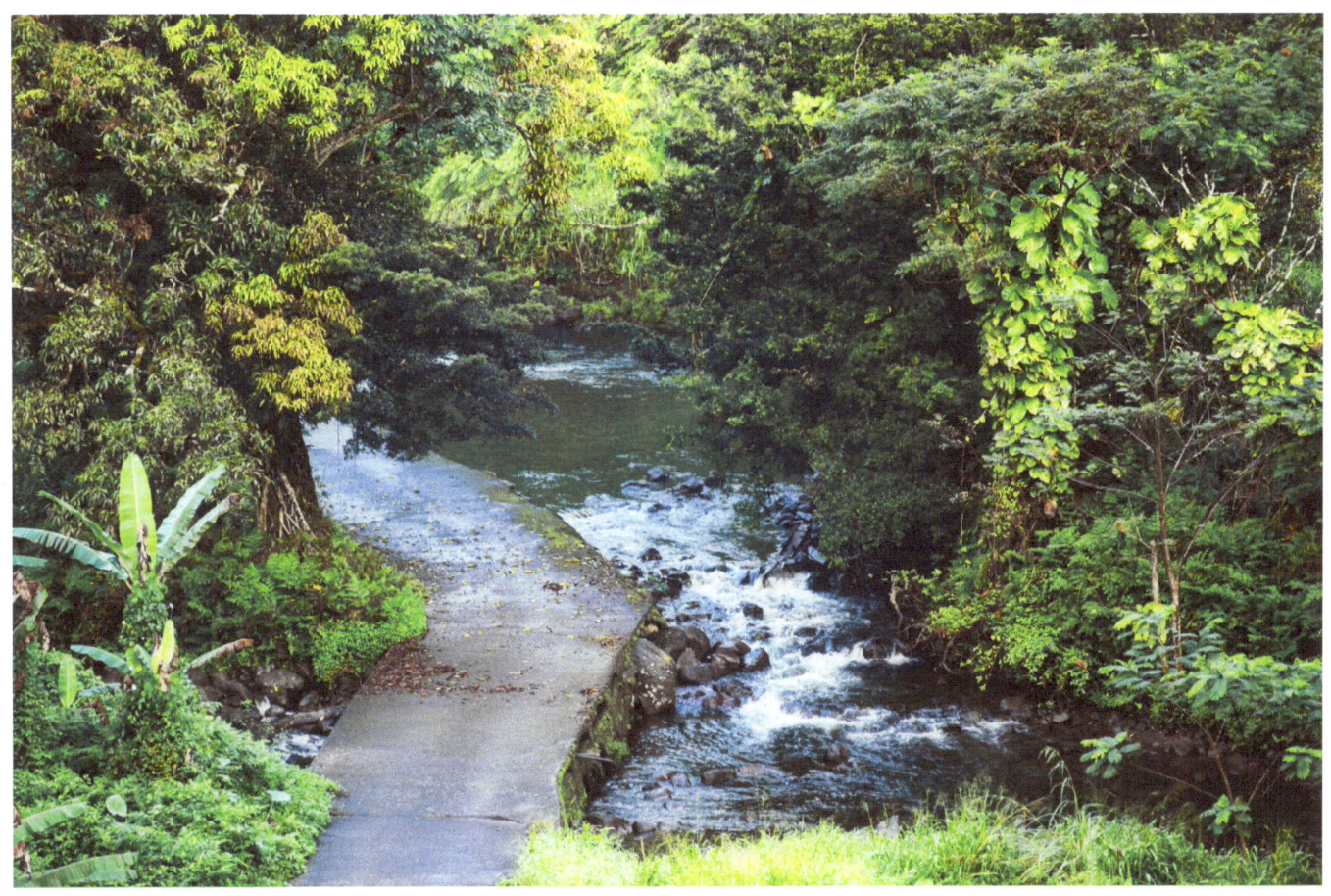

Summer Crossing   Molly Hart

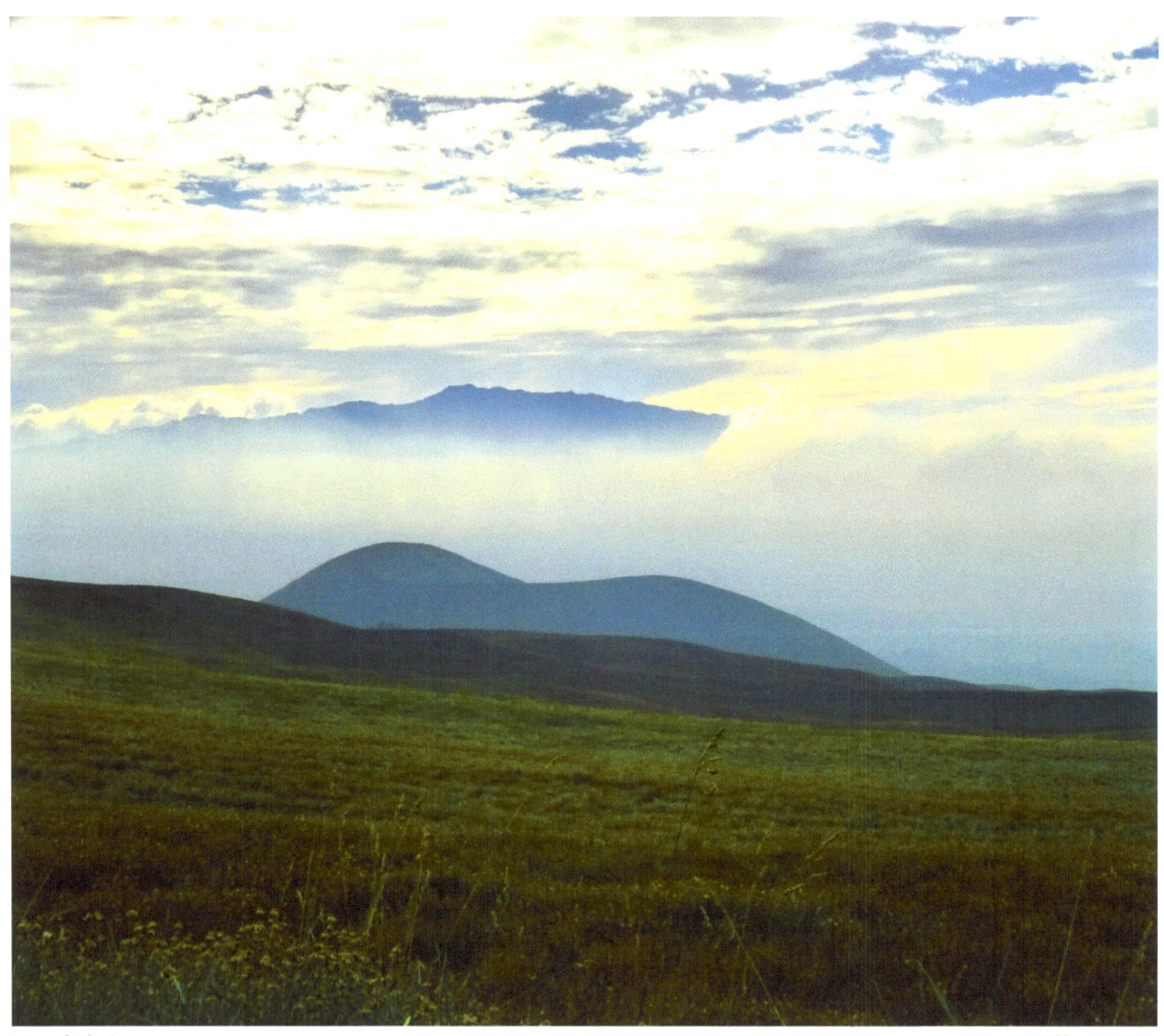

Hualālai

Molly Hart

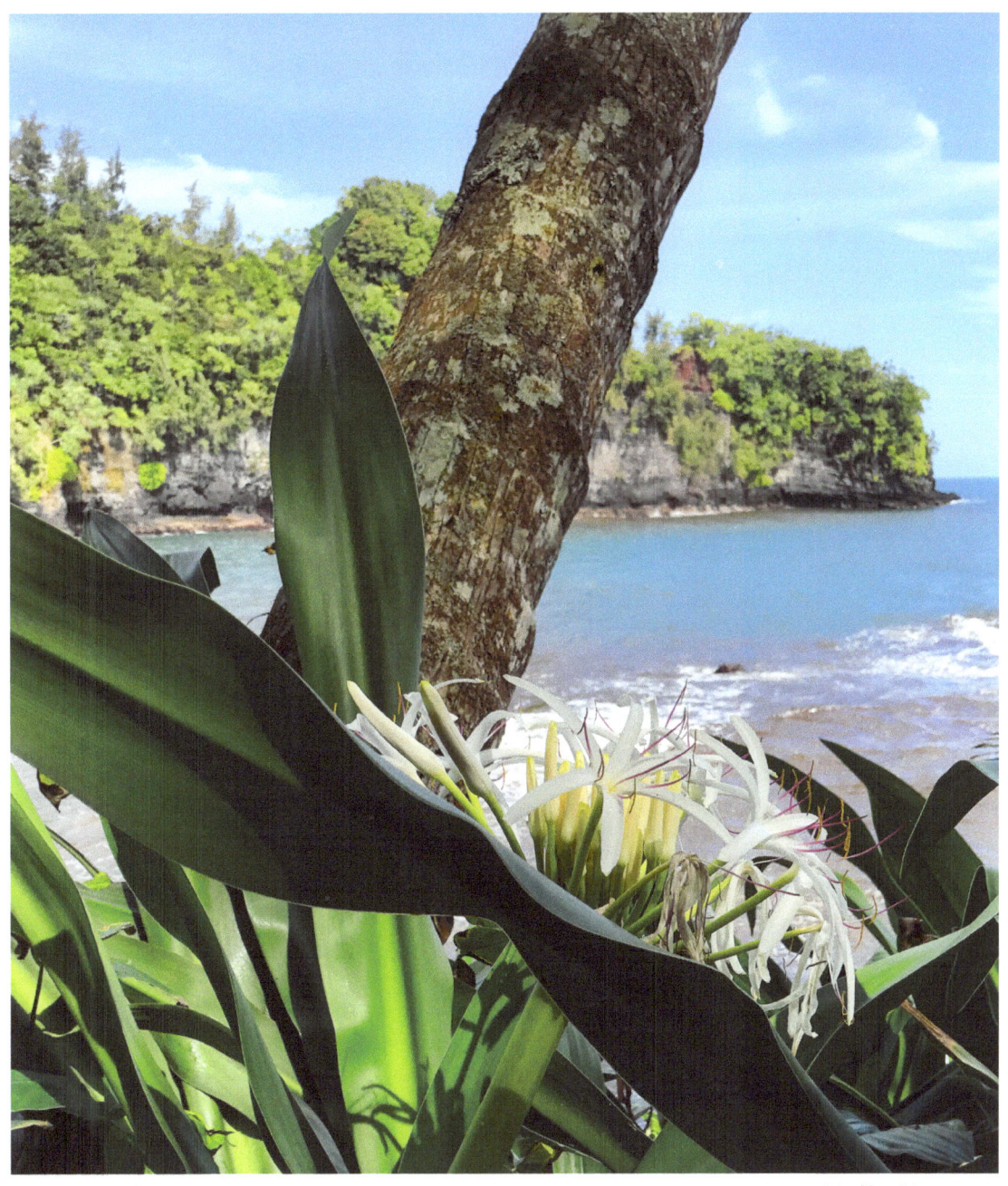

Onomea Bay   Molly Hart

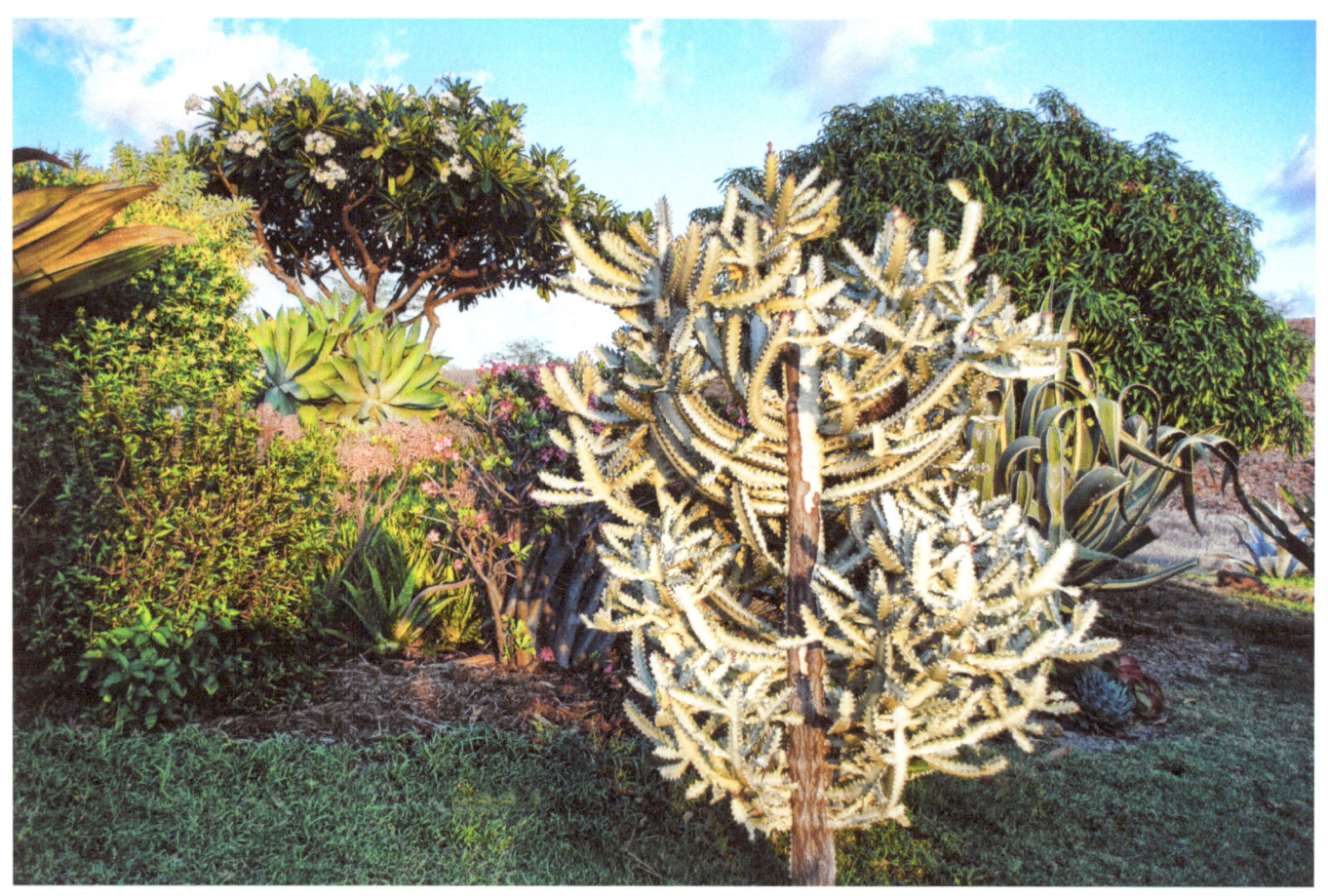

Kalia's Garden

Molly Hart

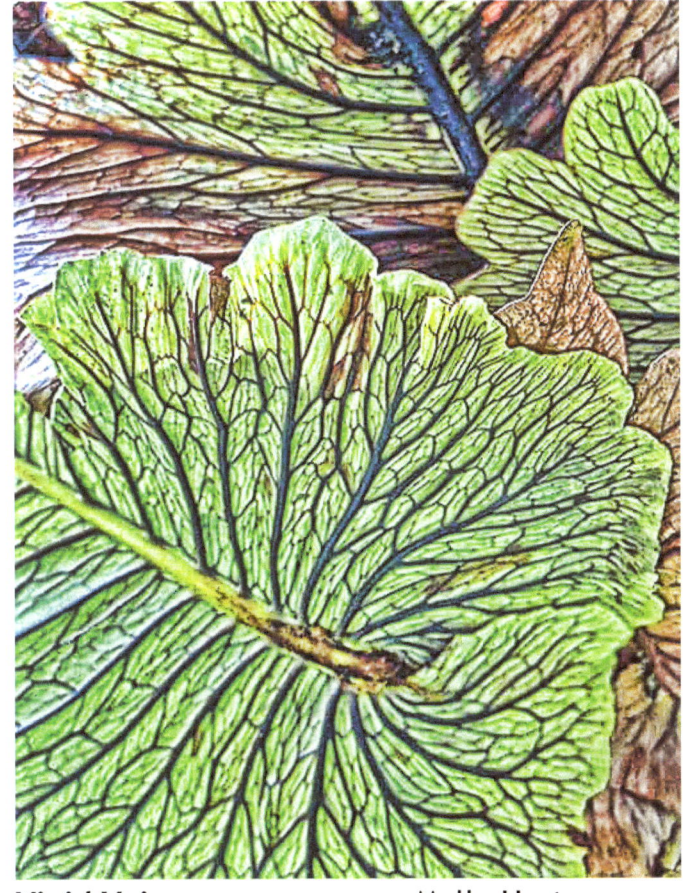

Vivid Veins   Molly Hart

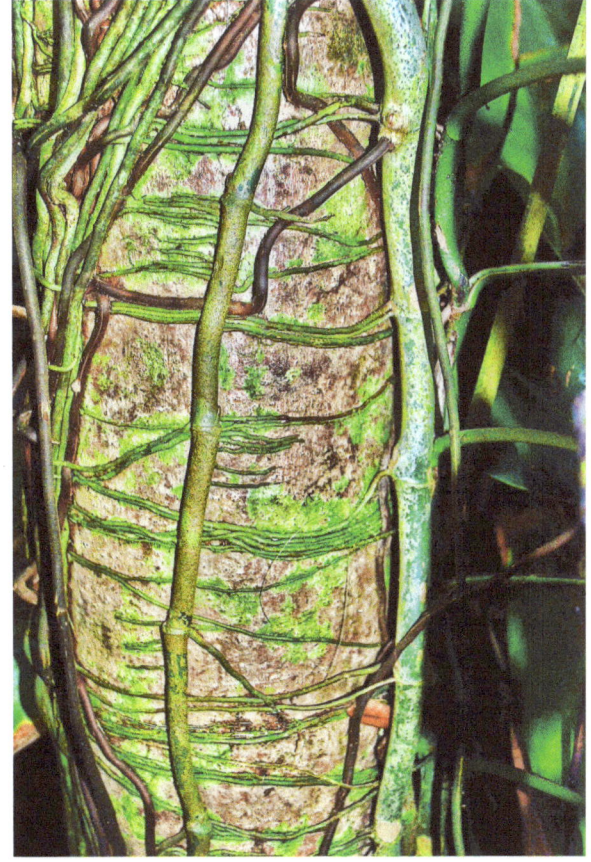

Bound   Molly Hart

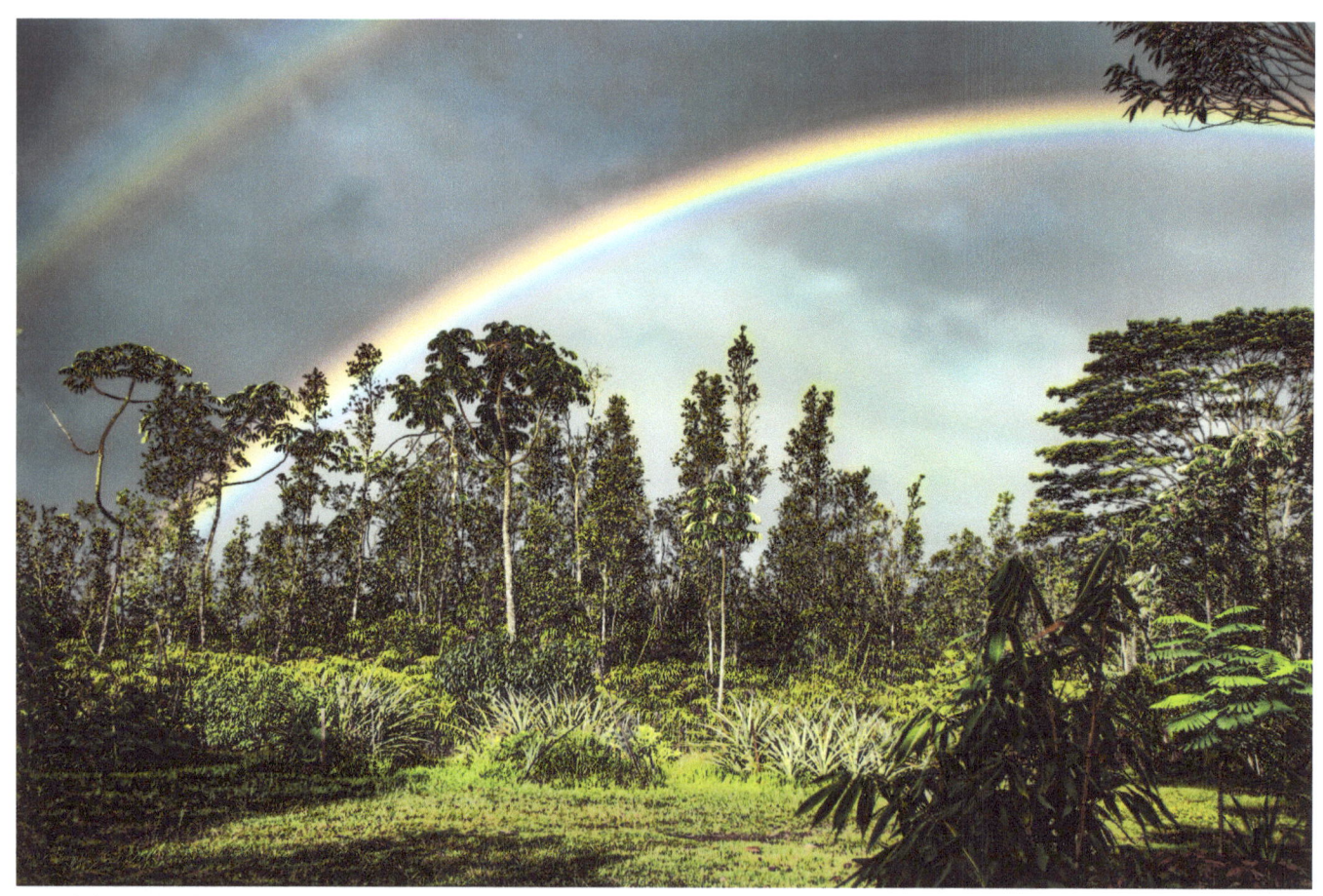

Double Rainbow

Molly Hart

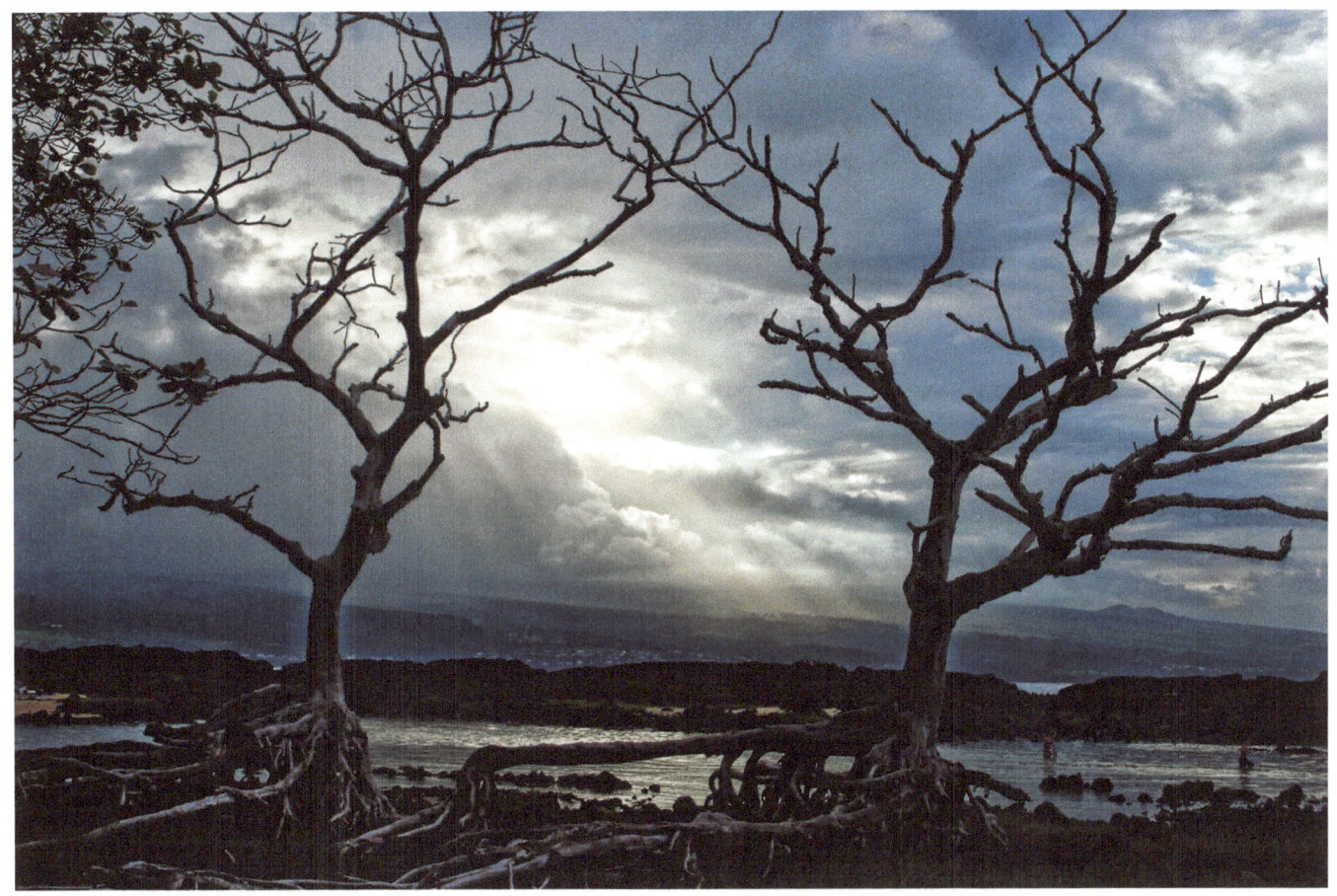

Dusk at Hilo Bay

Molly Hart

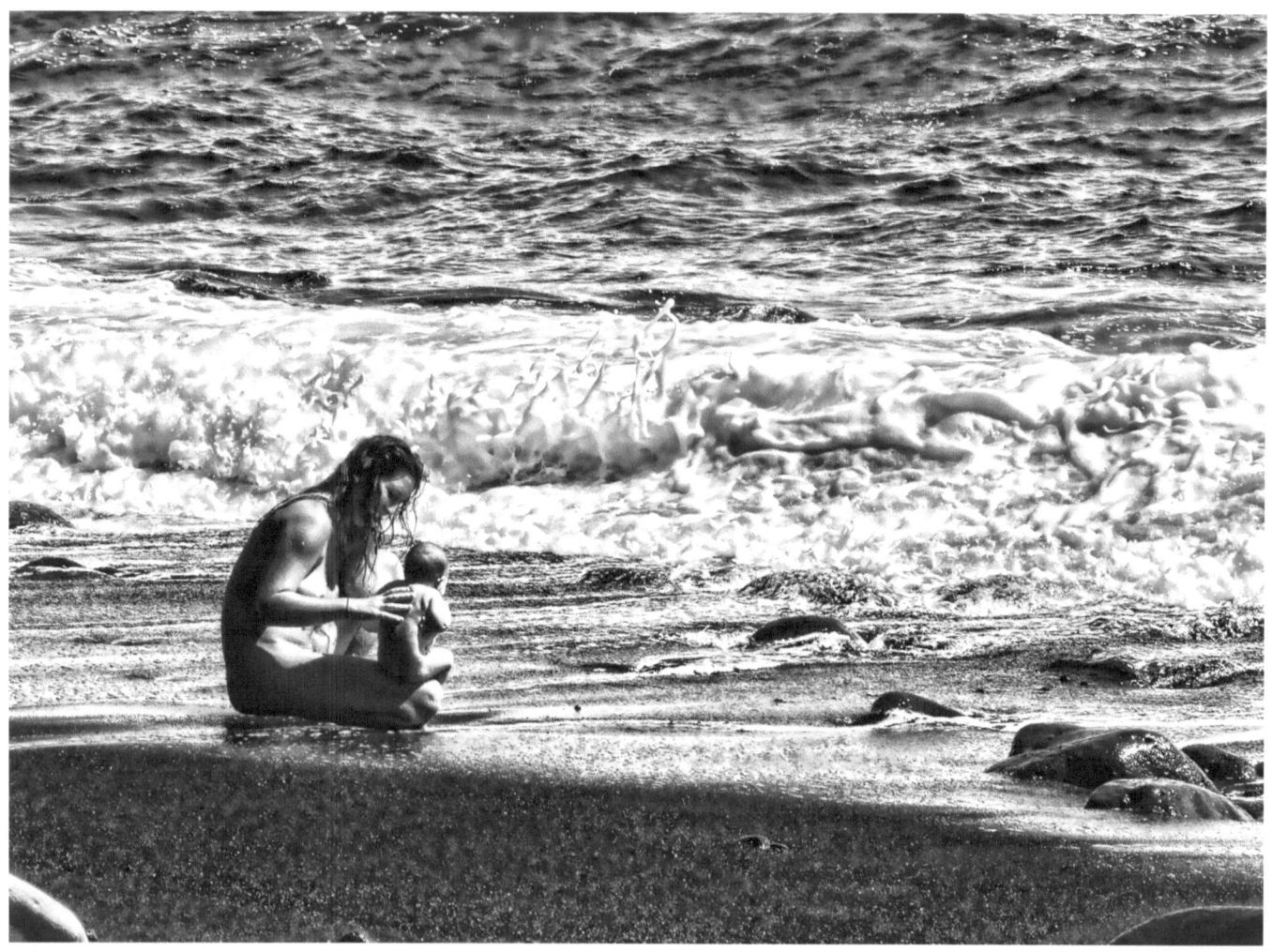

Christening   Molly Hart

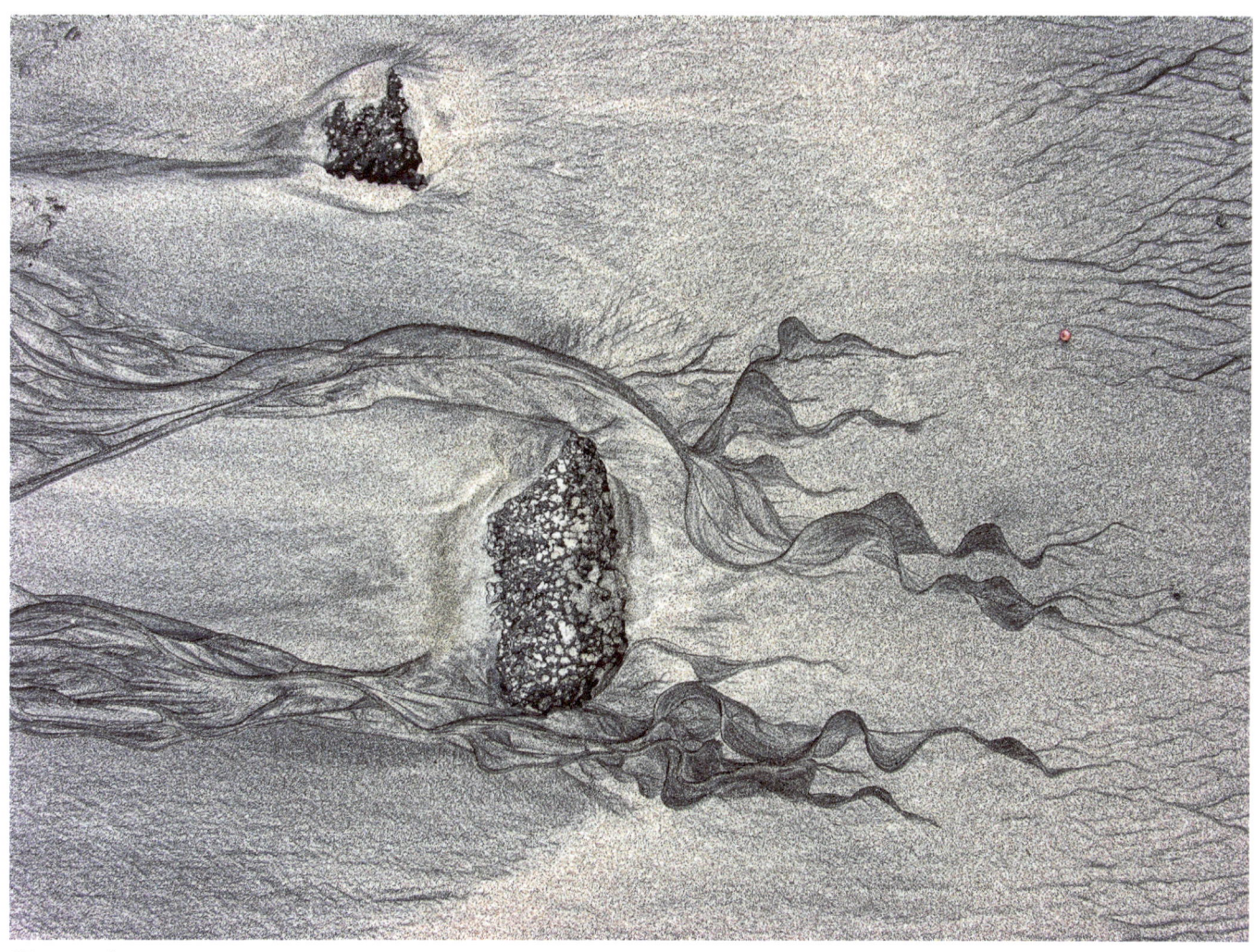

Tentacles

Molly Hart

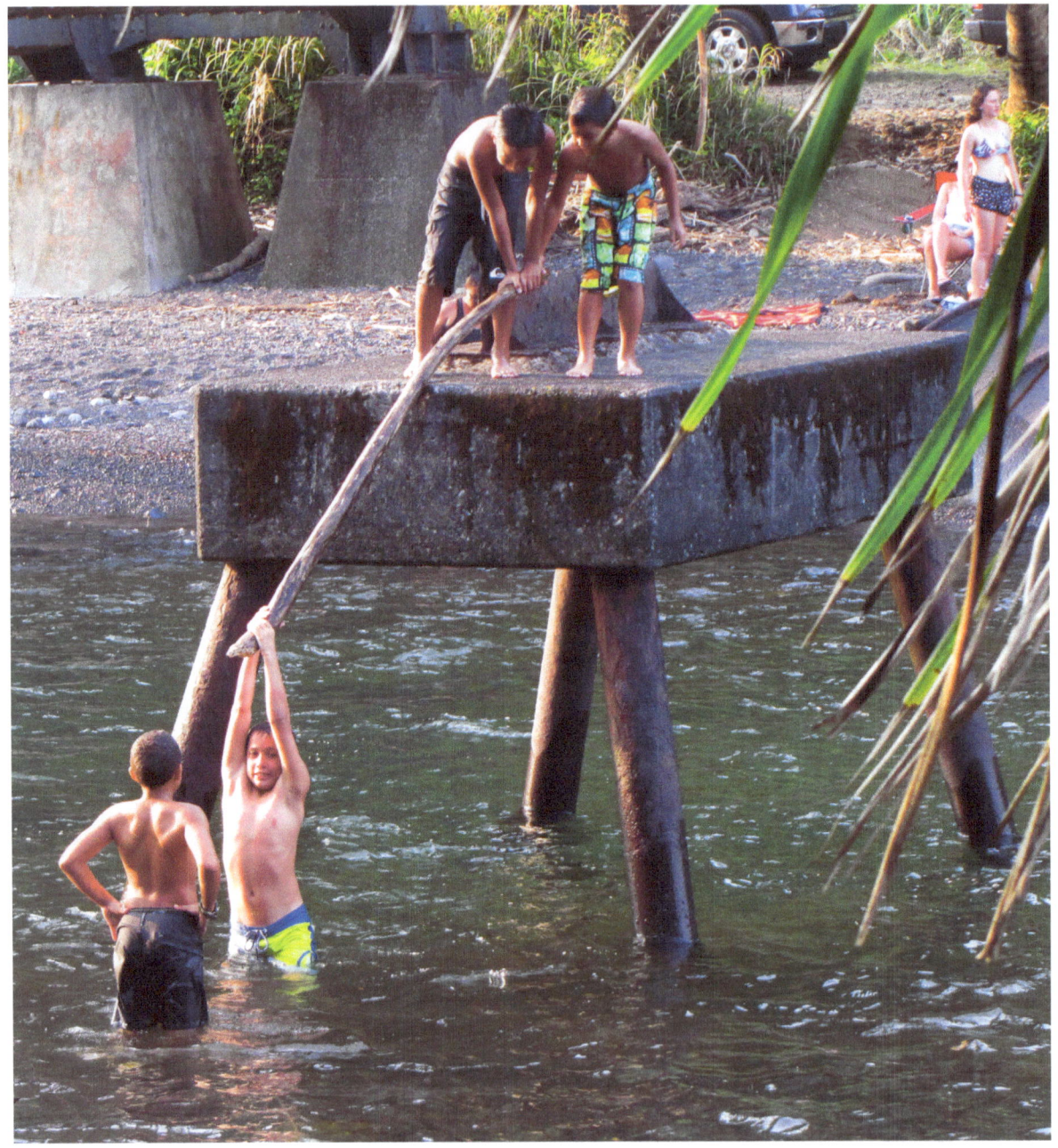

Play Time

Kelly Hart

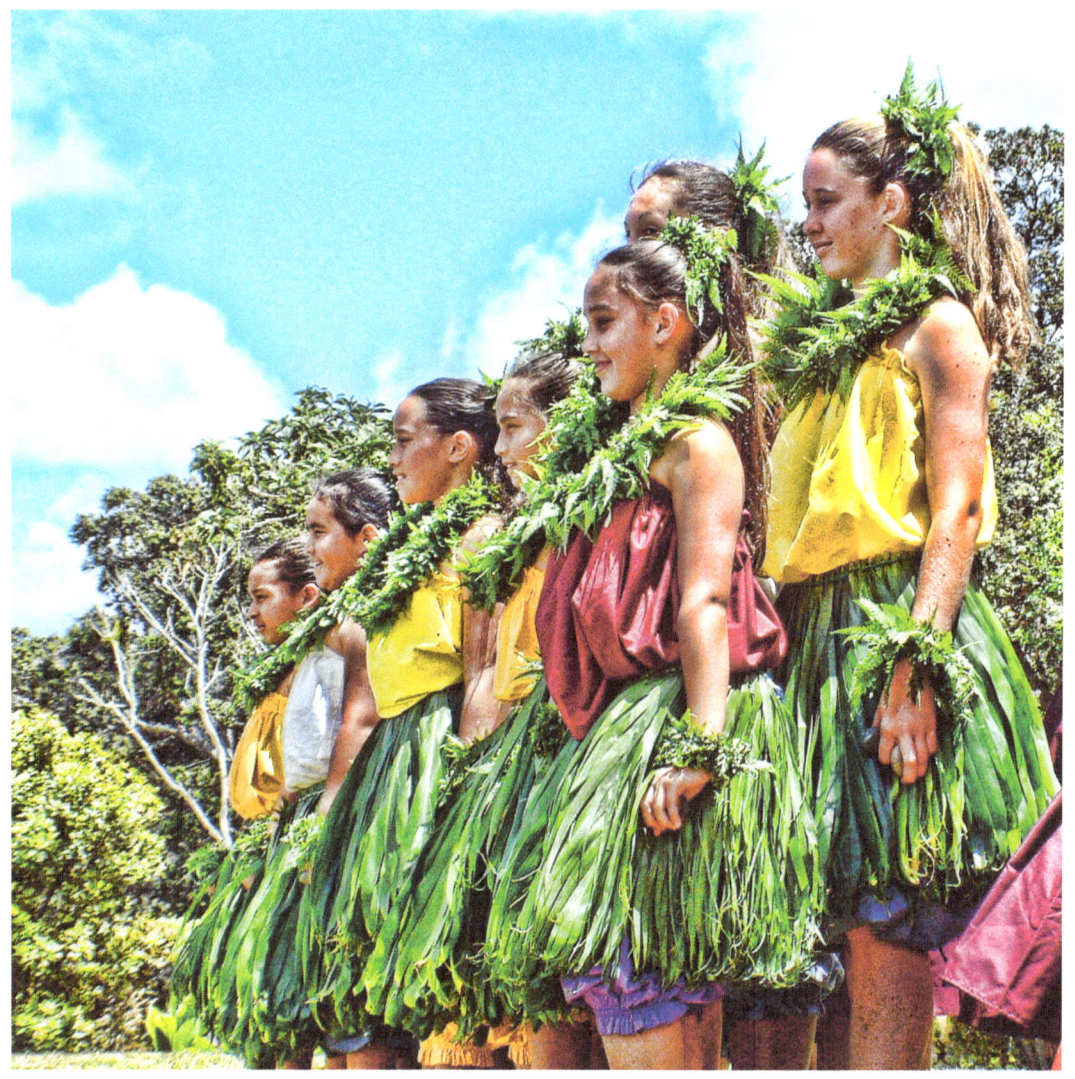

7 Dancers　　　　　　　　　　　　　　　　　　　　　　　Molly Hart

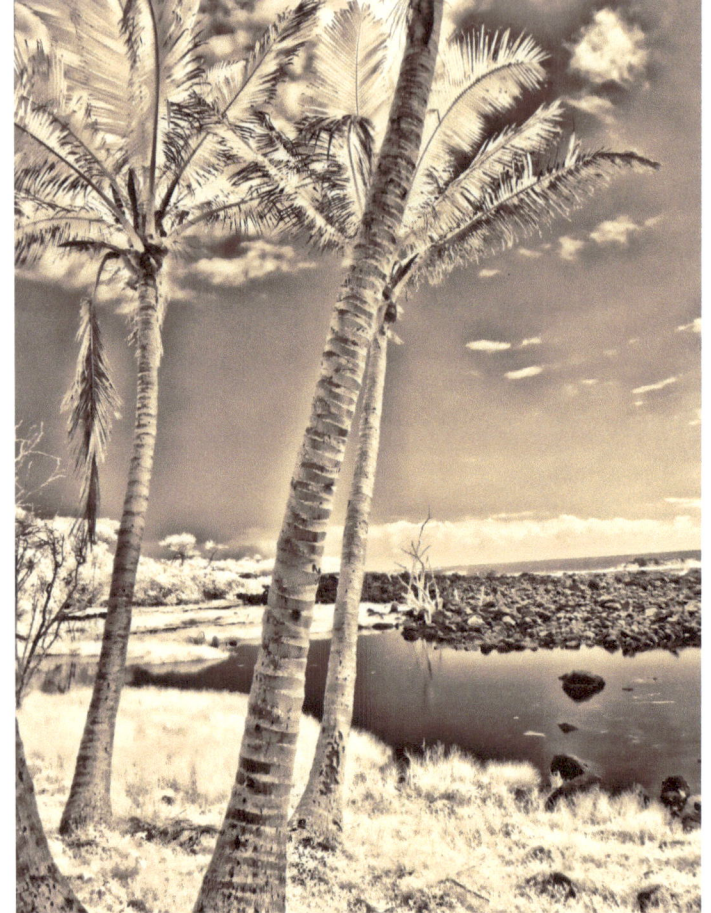

Hot Pond Palms   Molly Hart

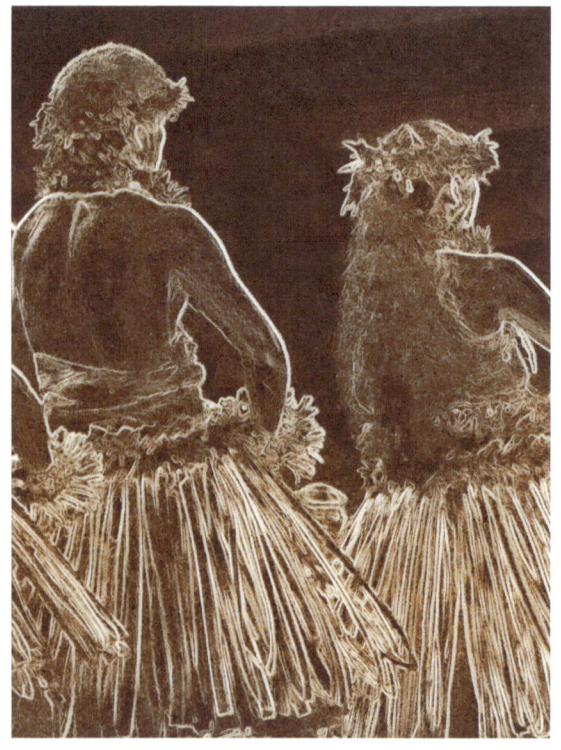

Looking Back   Molly Hart

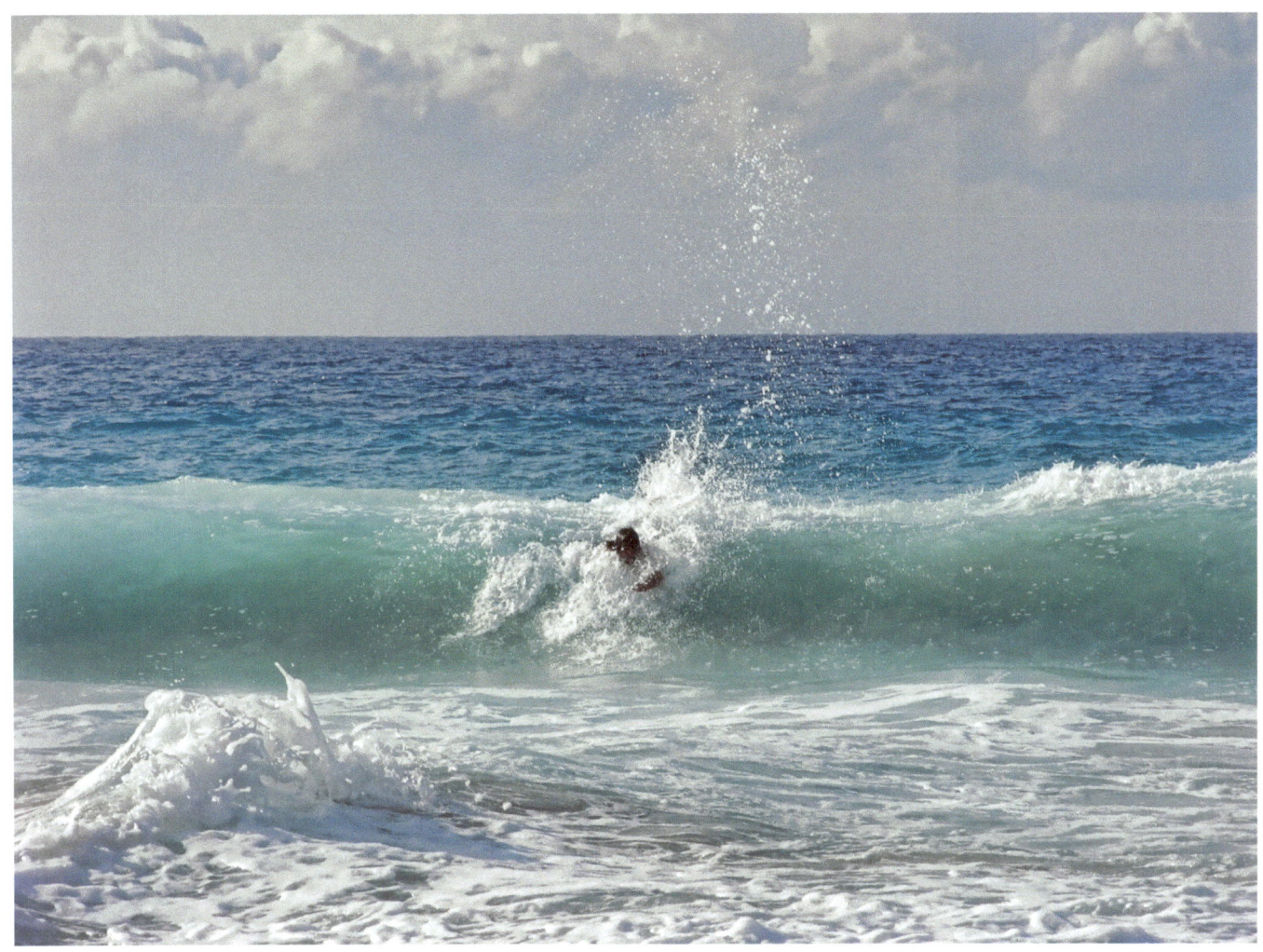

Body Surf

Molly Hart

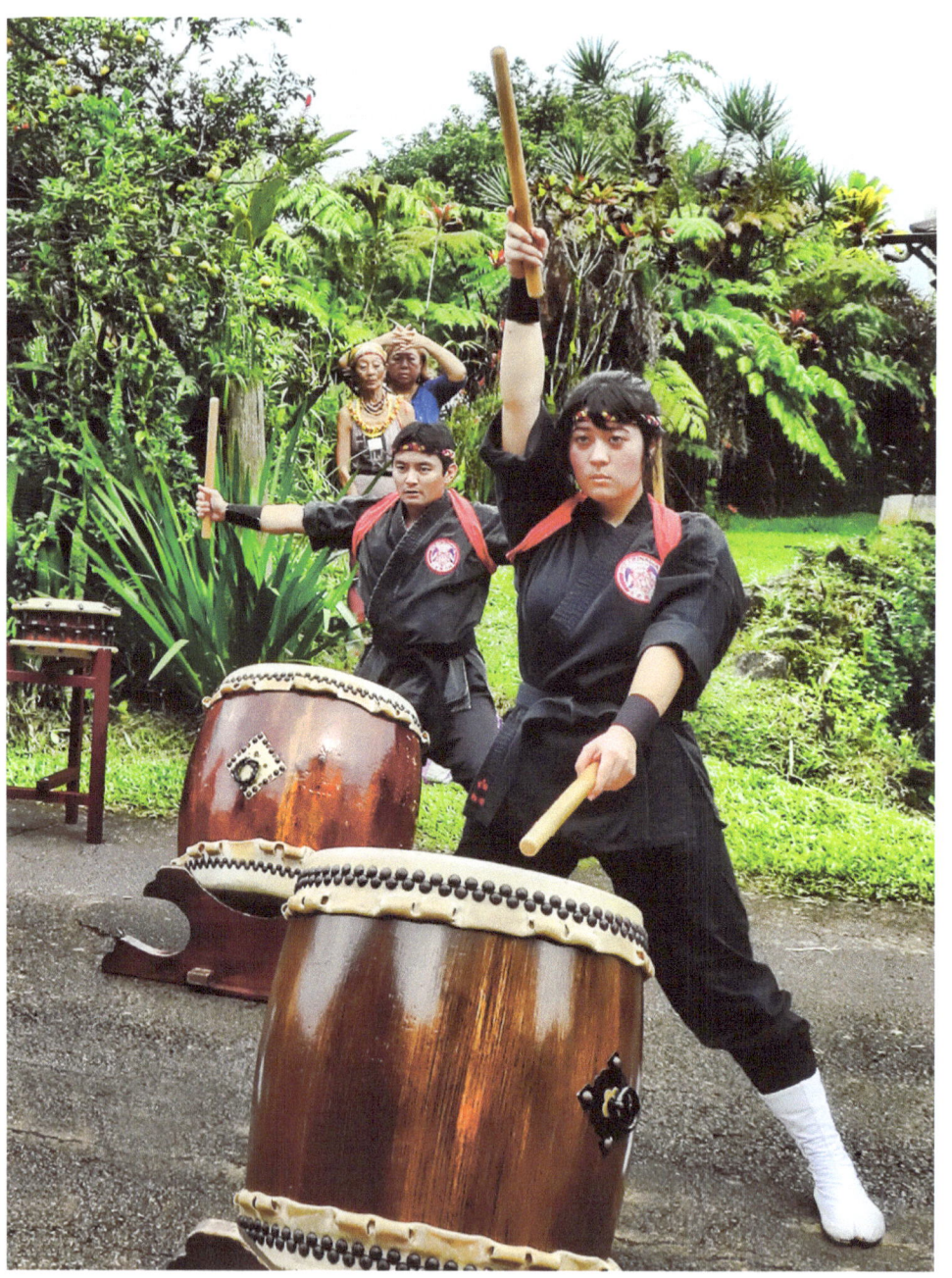

Dynamic Intent   Molly Hart

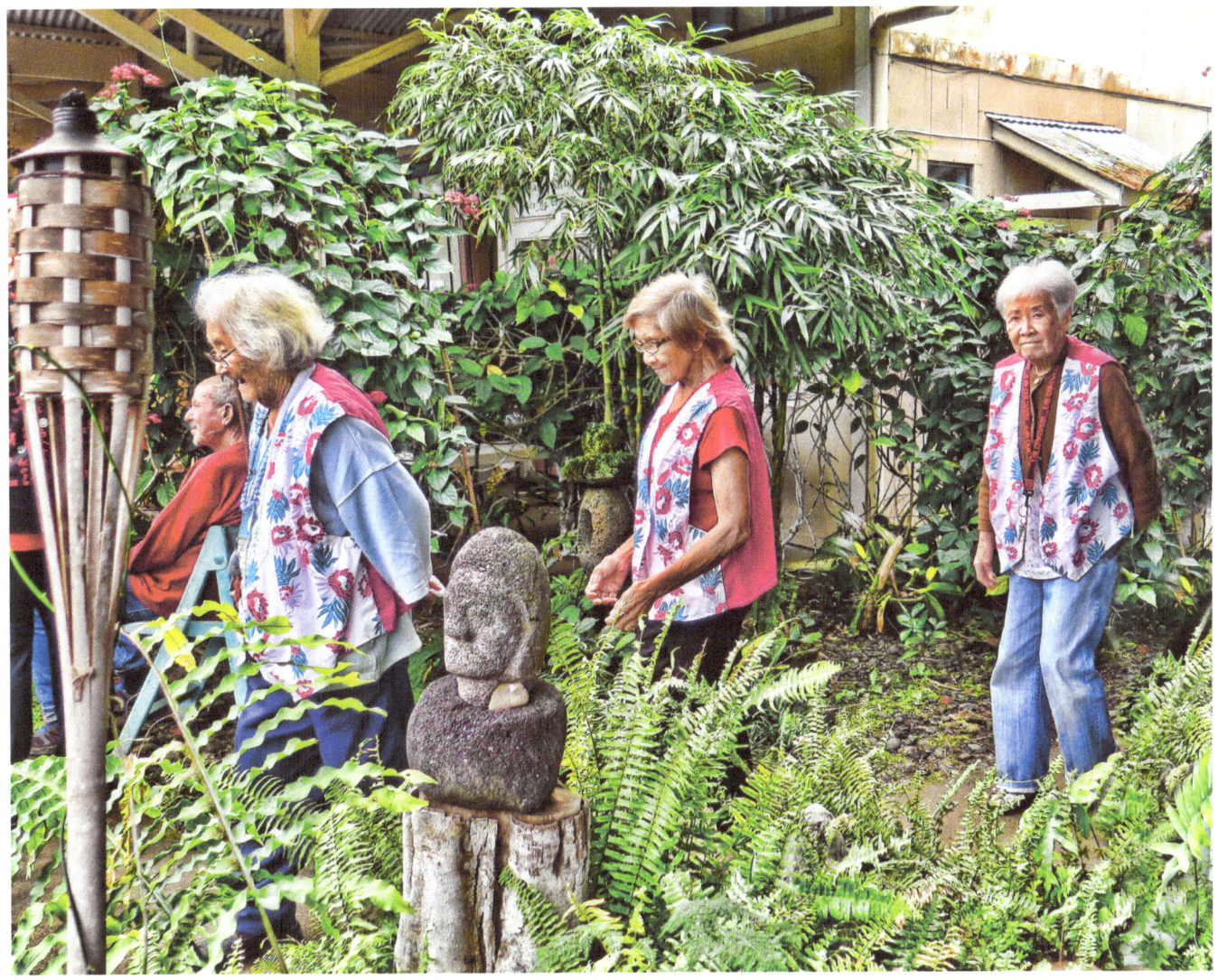

Kapuna

Molly Hart

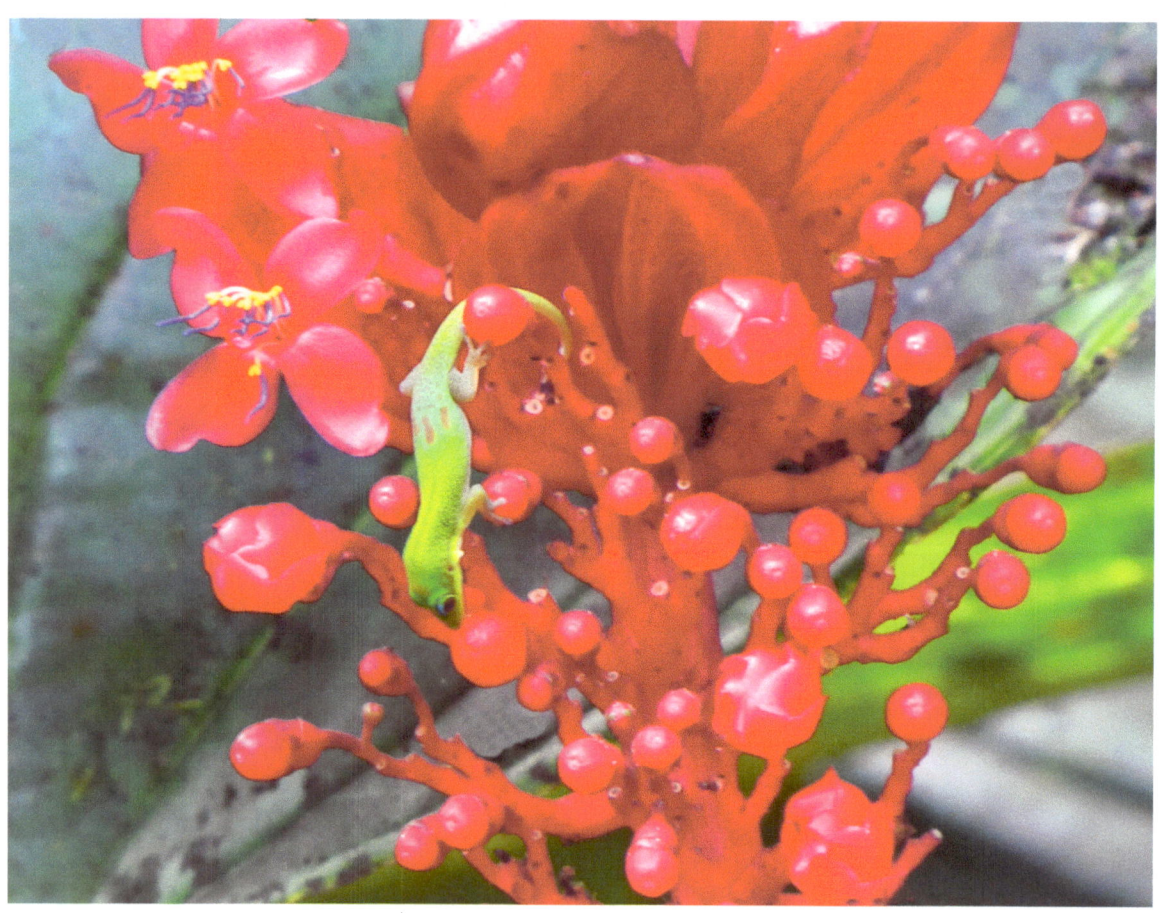

Lizzy

Kelly Hart

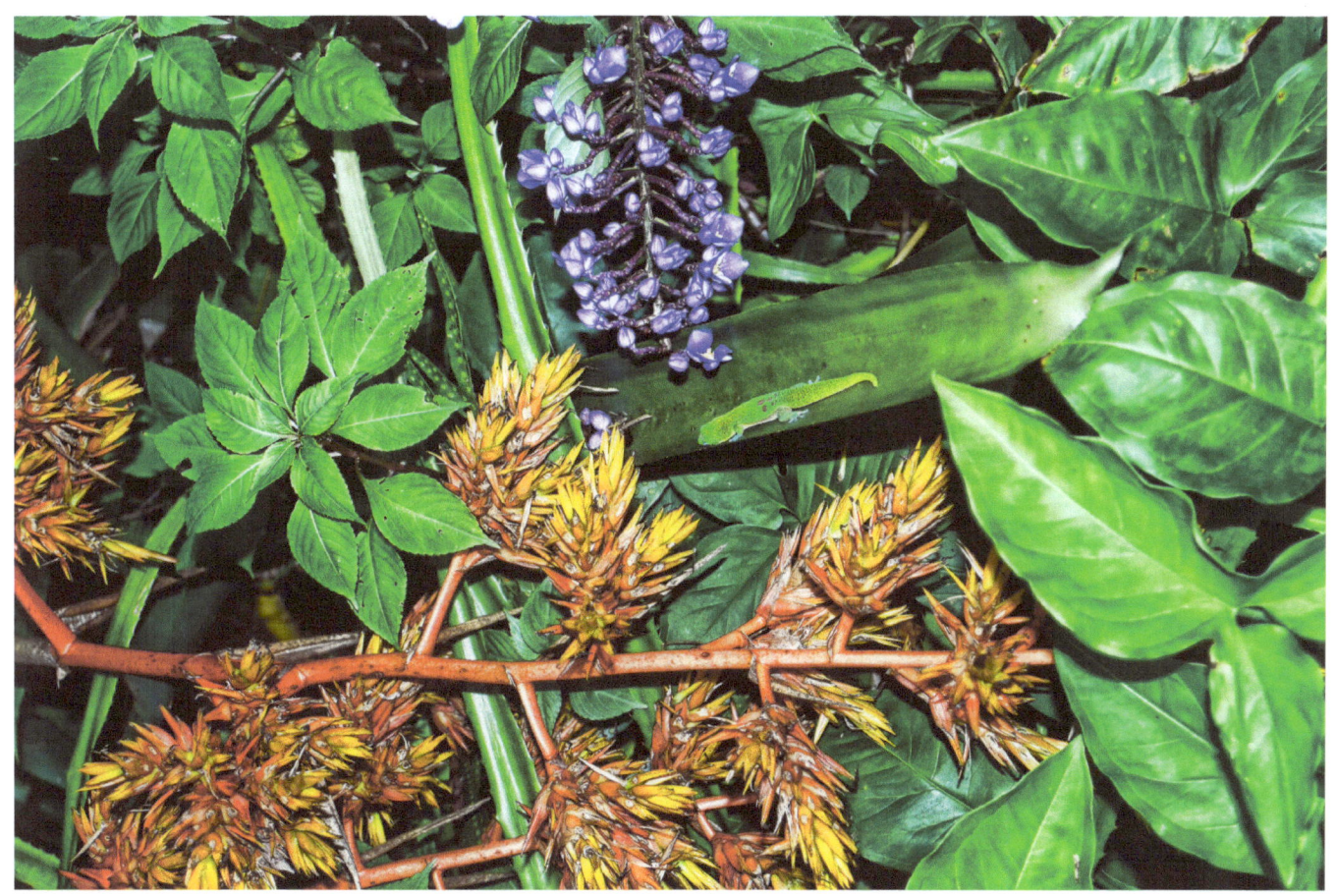

Diversity

Molly Hart

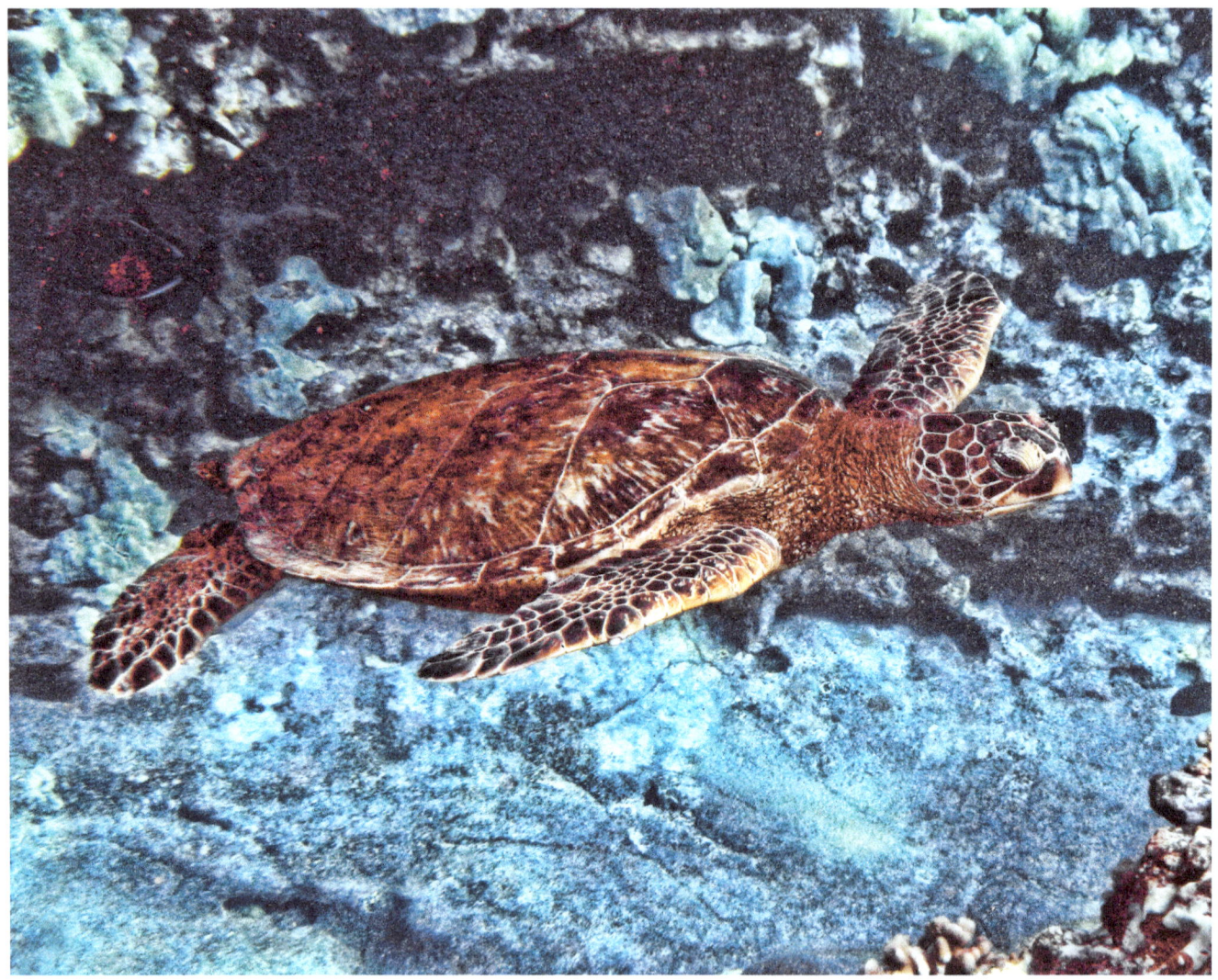

Ho'okena Honu

Molly Hart

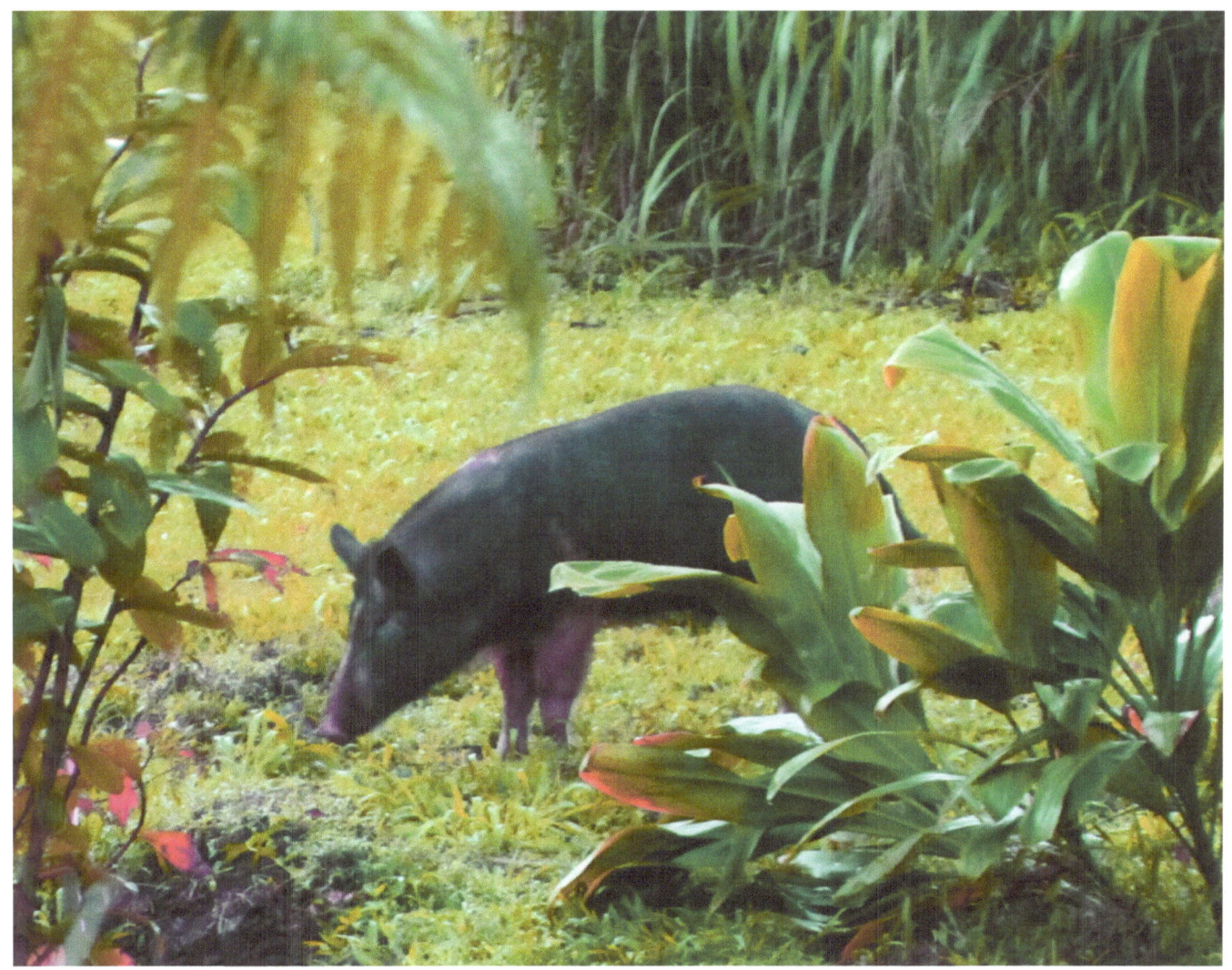

Feral Pig

Kelly Hart

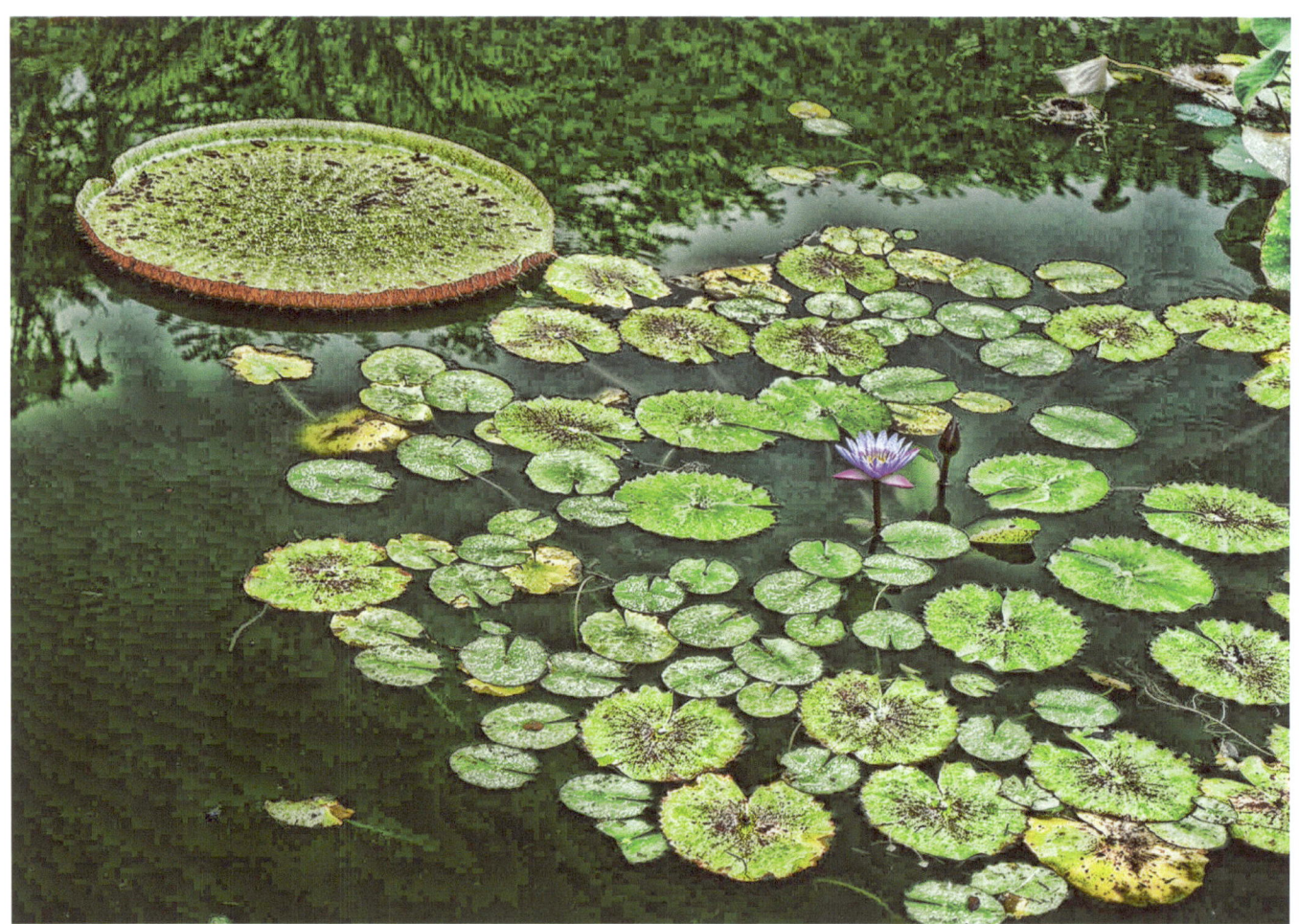

Pana'ewa

Molly Hart

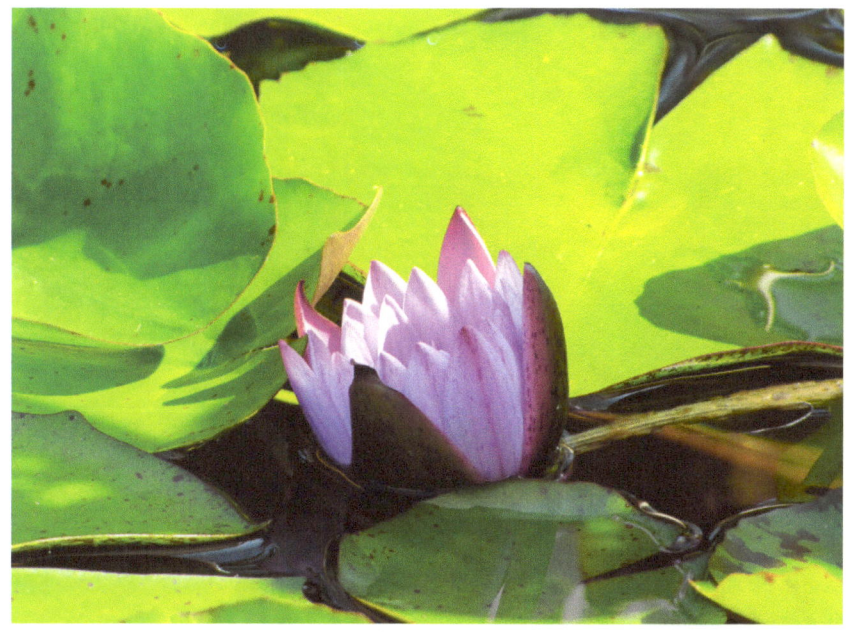

Water Lily   Kelly Hart

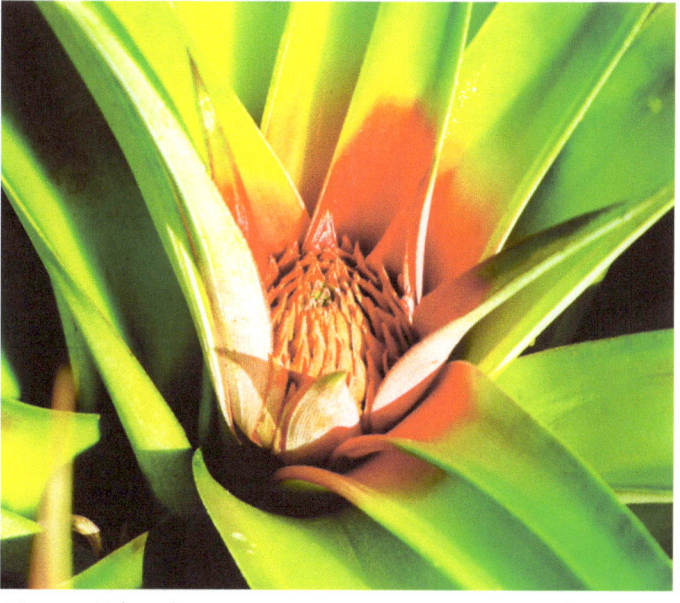

Heart Throb   Kelly Hart

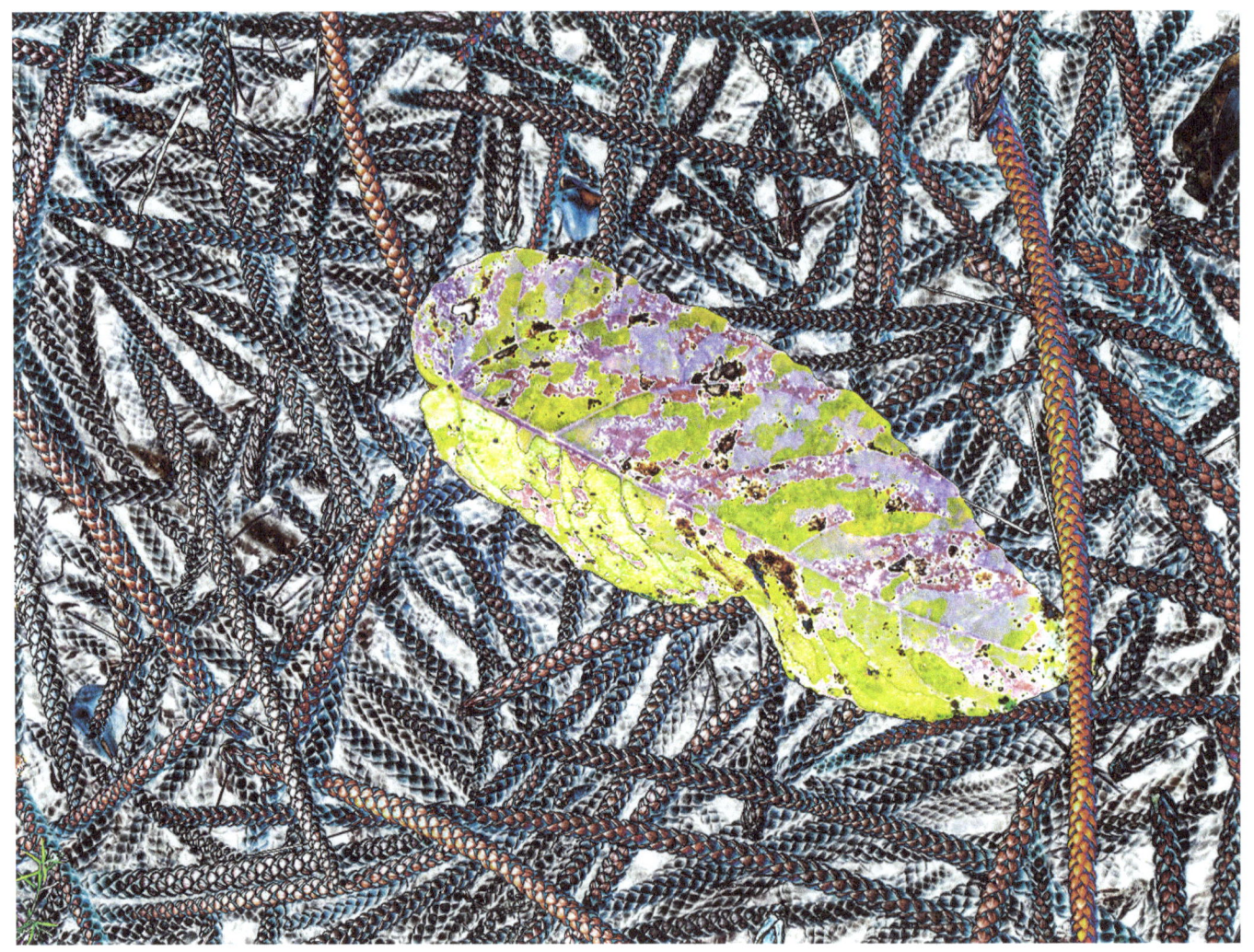

Bed of Needles

Molly Hart

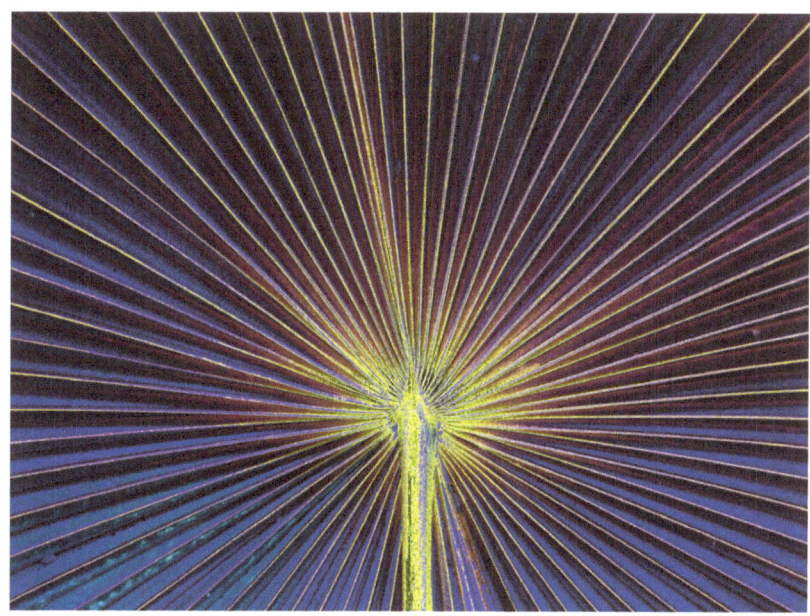

Fan   Molly Hart

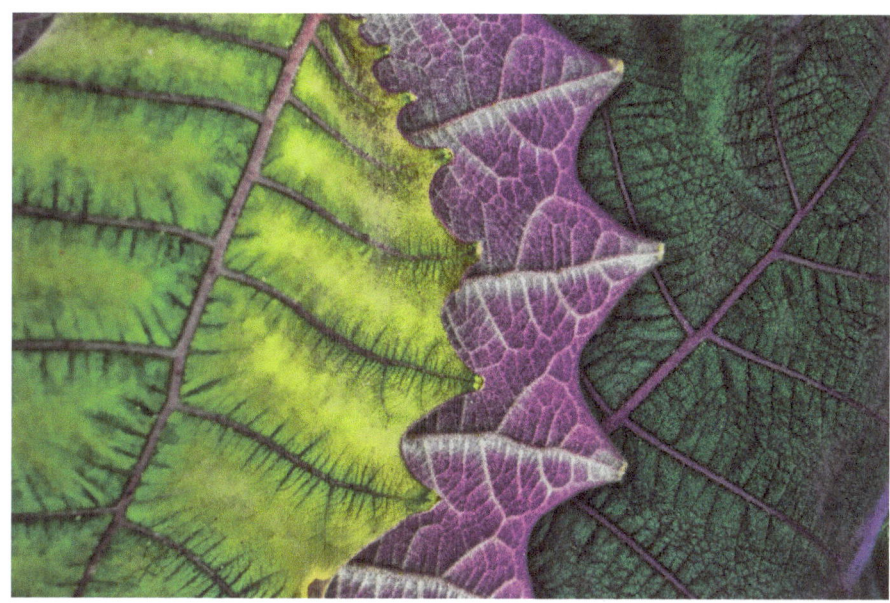

Spicify   Molly Hart

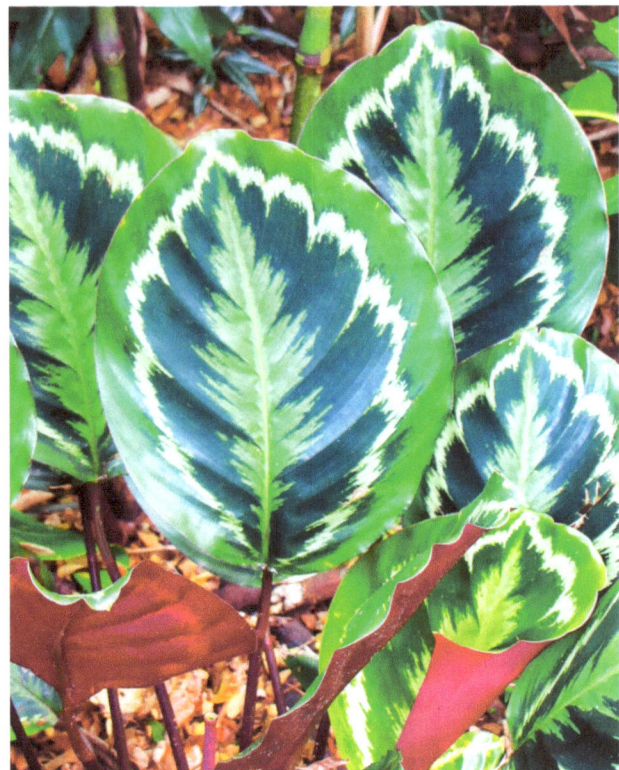

Brushed Kelly Hart

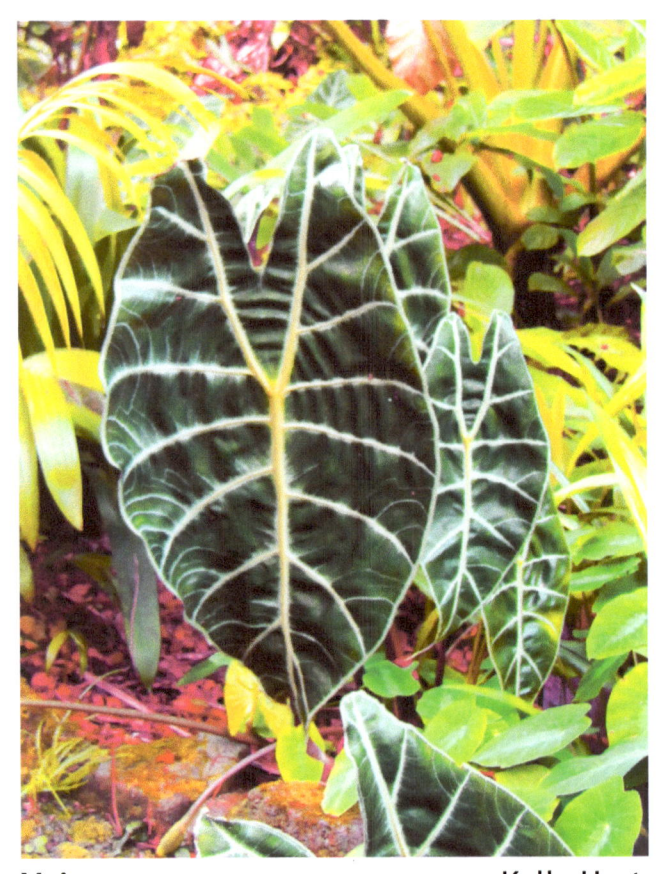

Veins Kelly Hart

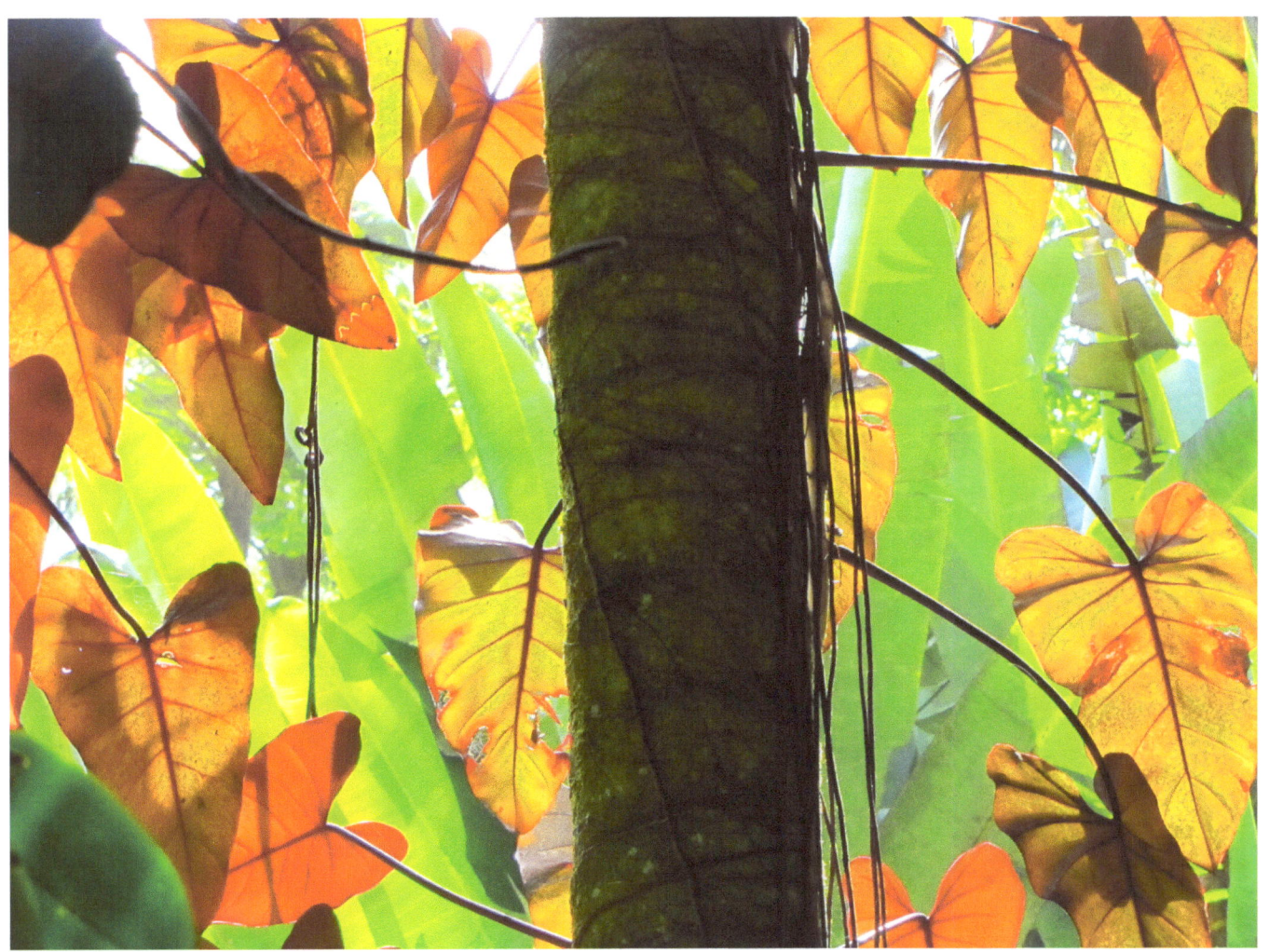

Golden Glory   Kelly Hart

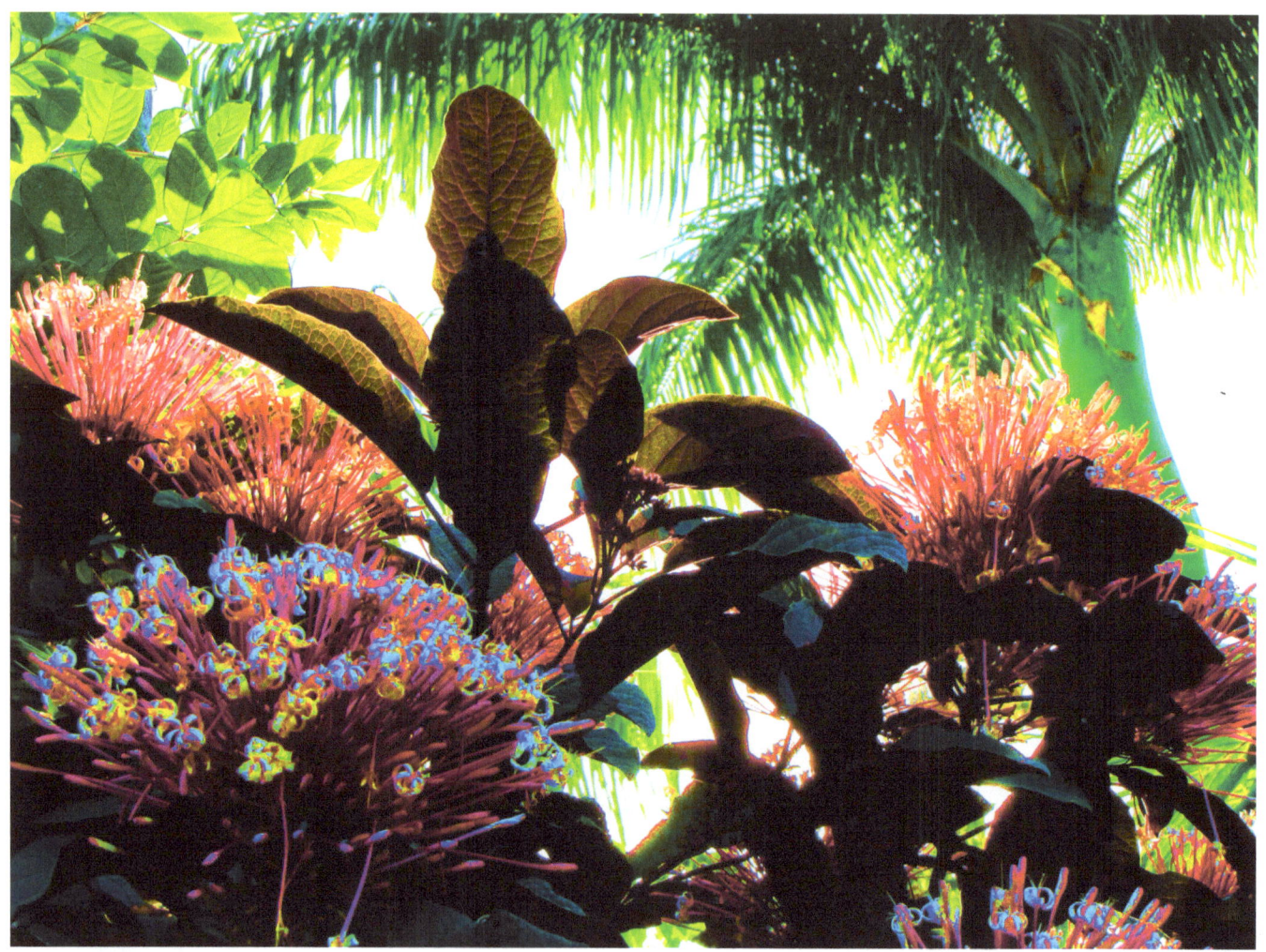

Towering Flowers   Kelly Hart

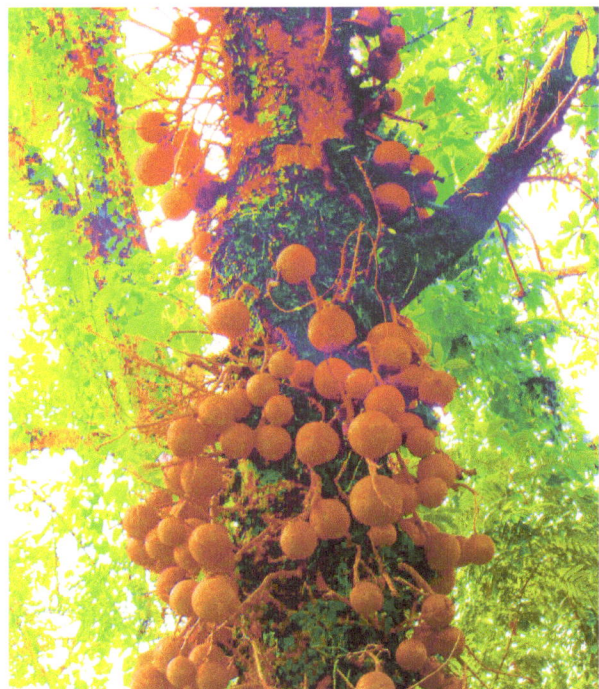

Dangles   Kelly Hart

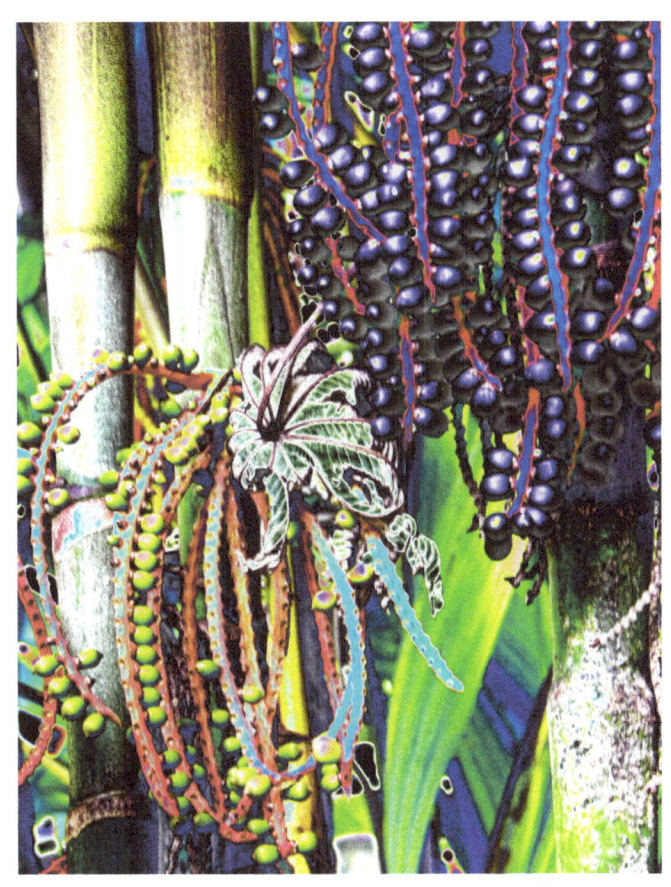

Jungle Jewels   Molly Hart

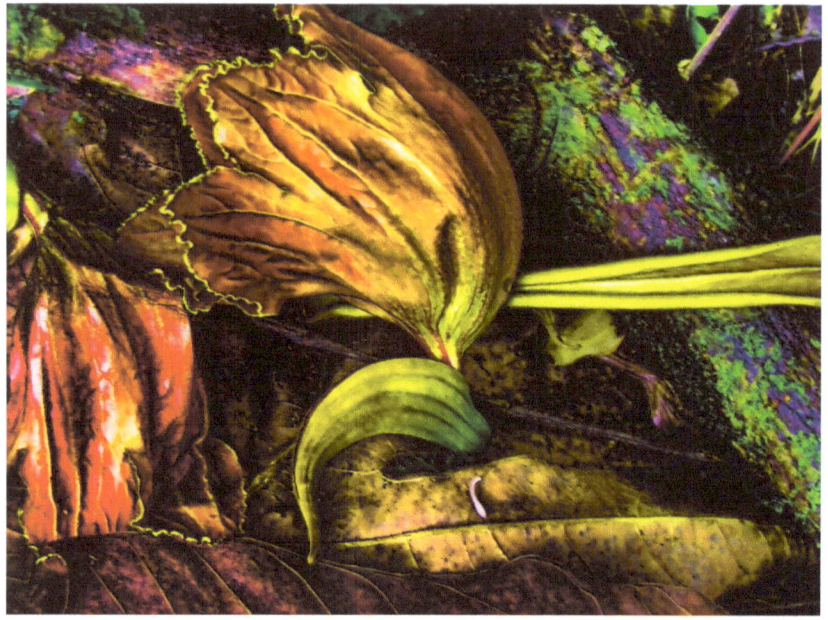

Glow in the Dark　　　　　　　　　　Molly Hart

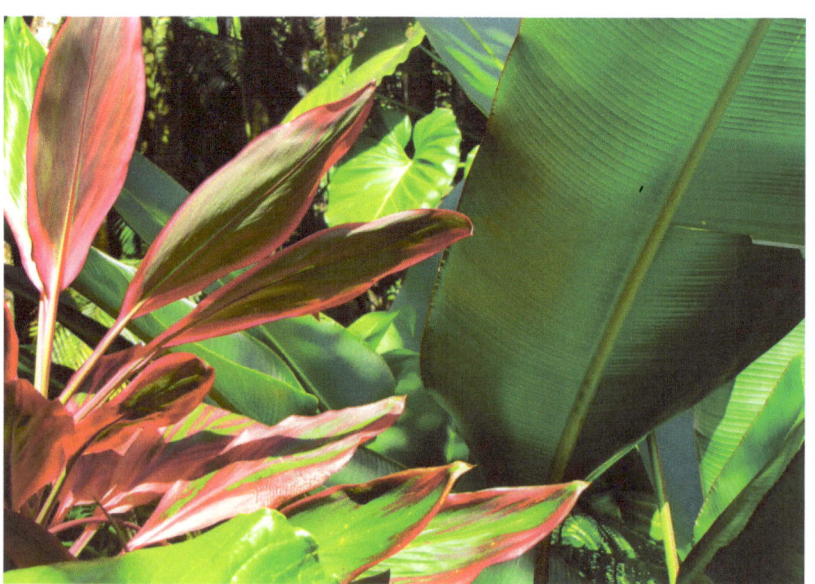

Fire Light　　　　　　　　　　Kelly Hart

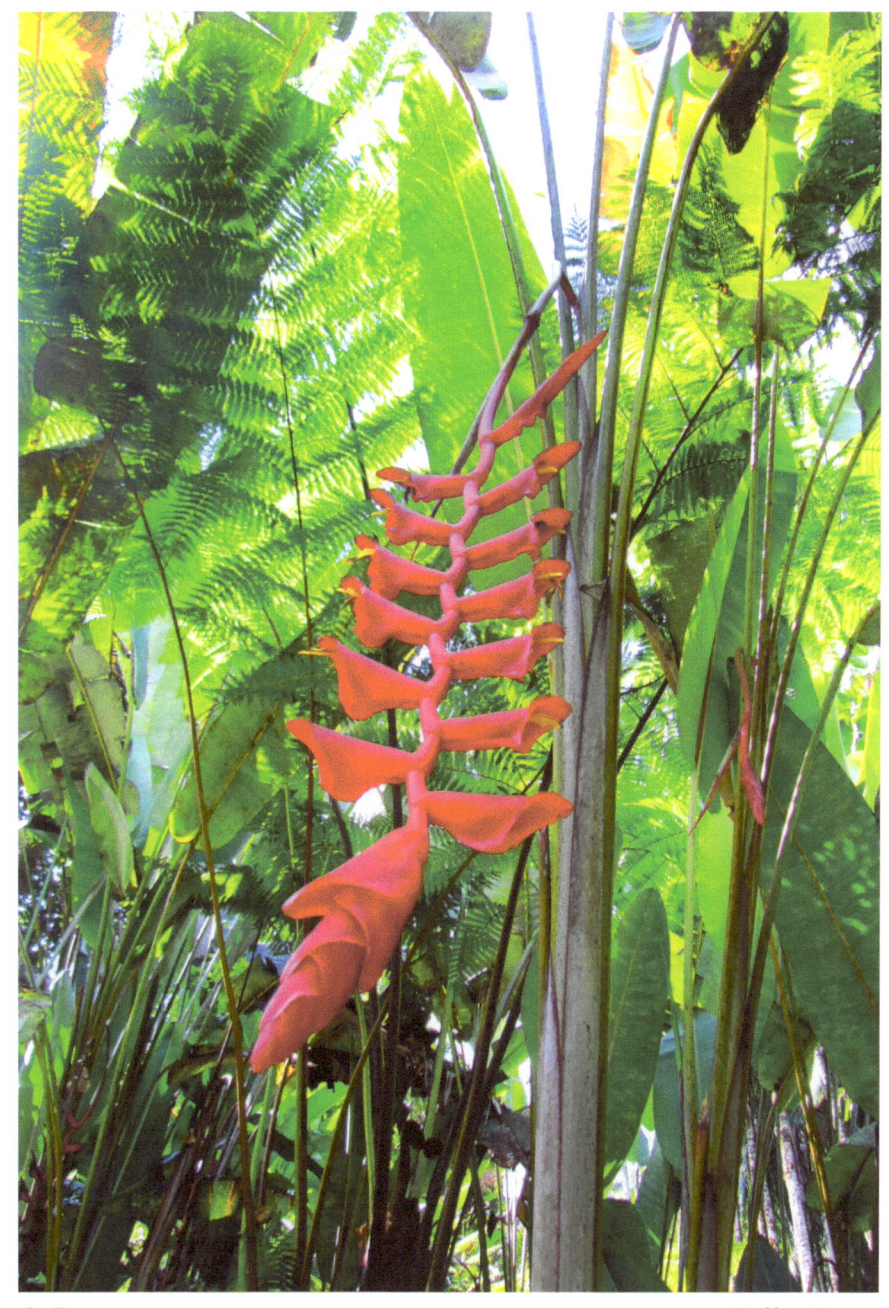

3-D   Kelly Hart

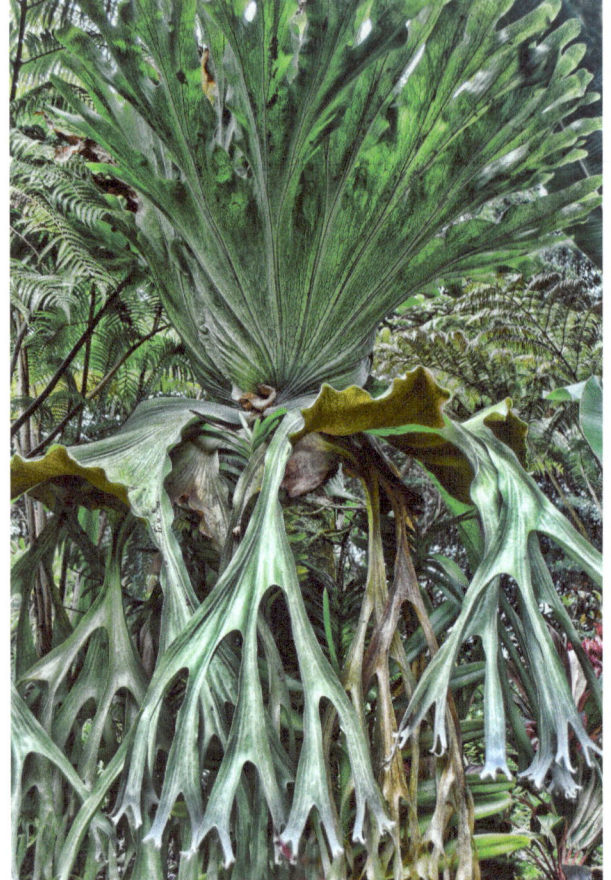

Surreal   Molly Hart

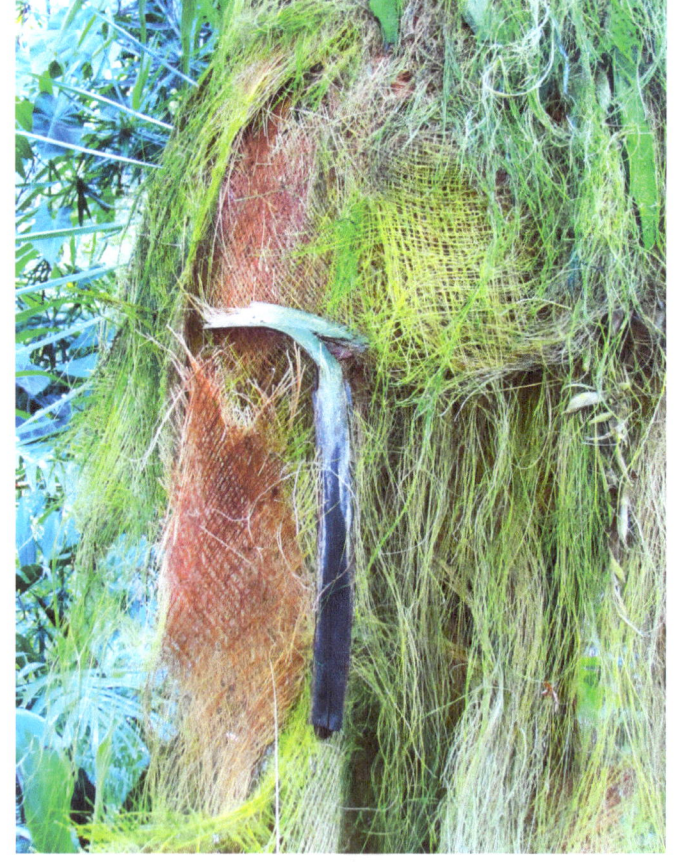

Fiber   Kelly Hart

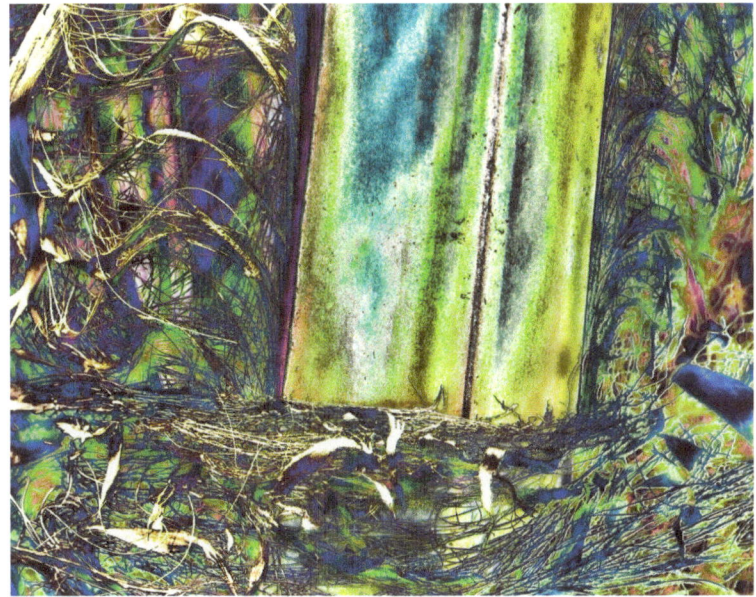

Enveloped   Molly Hart

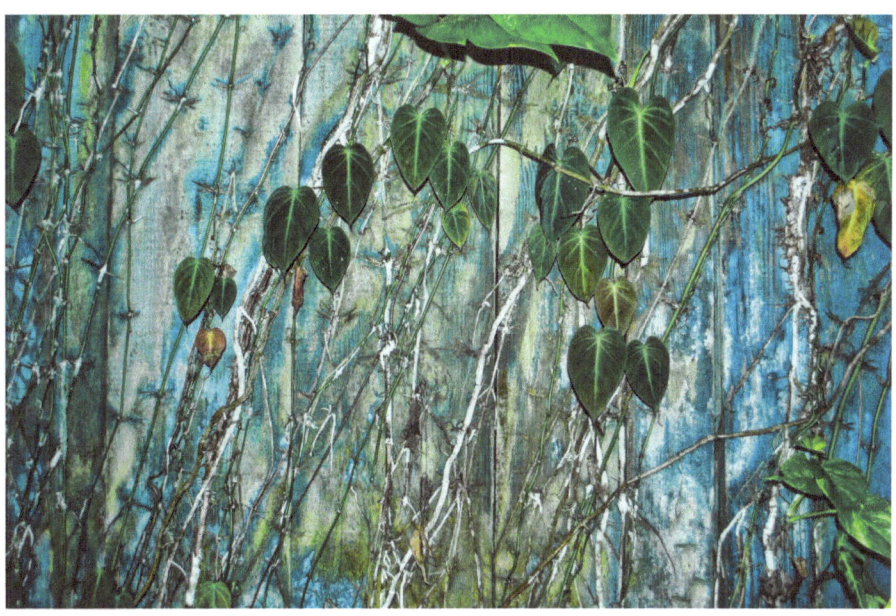

Vine Pallete   Molly Hart

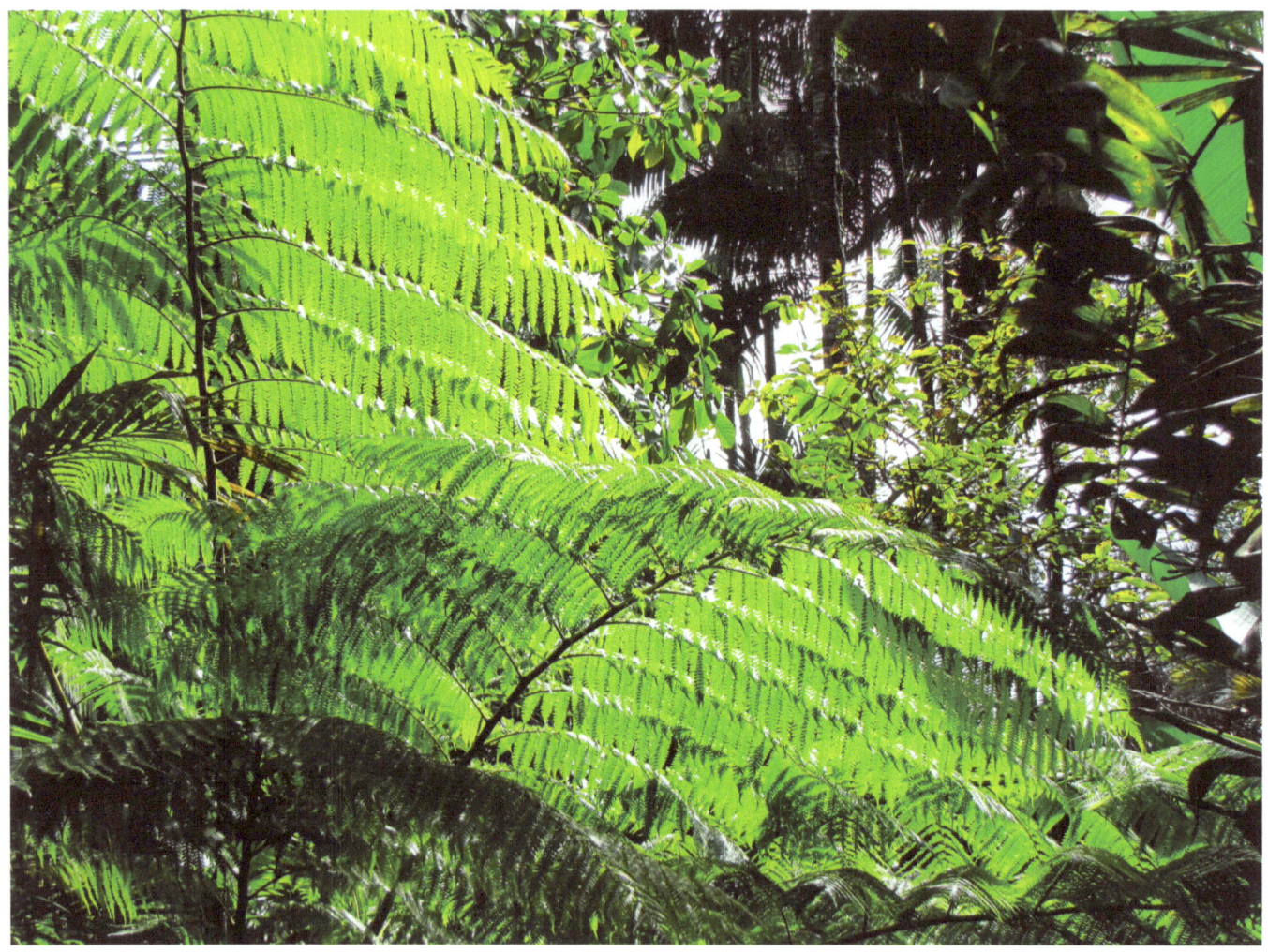

Delicate Patterns

Kelly Hart

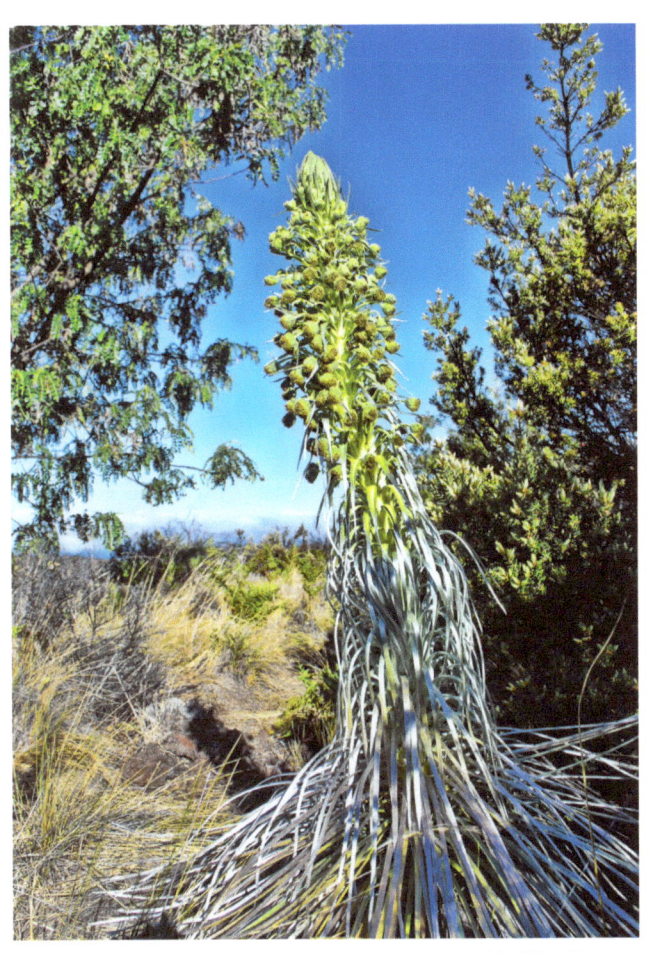

Silversword Molly Hart

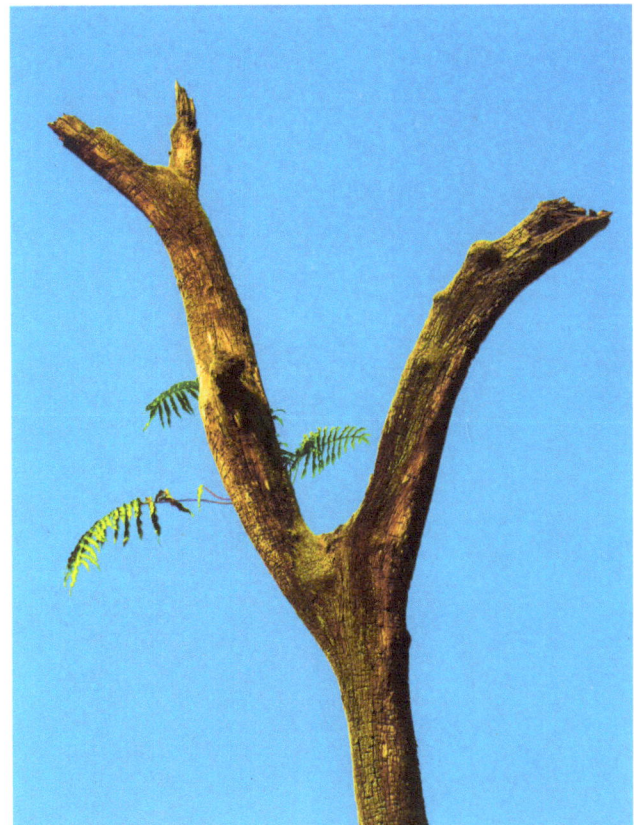

Tree Top Kelly Hart

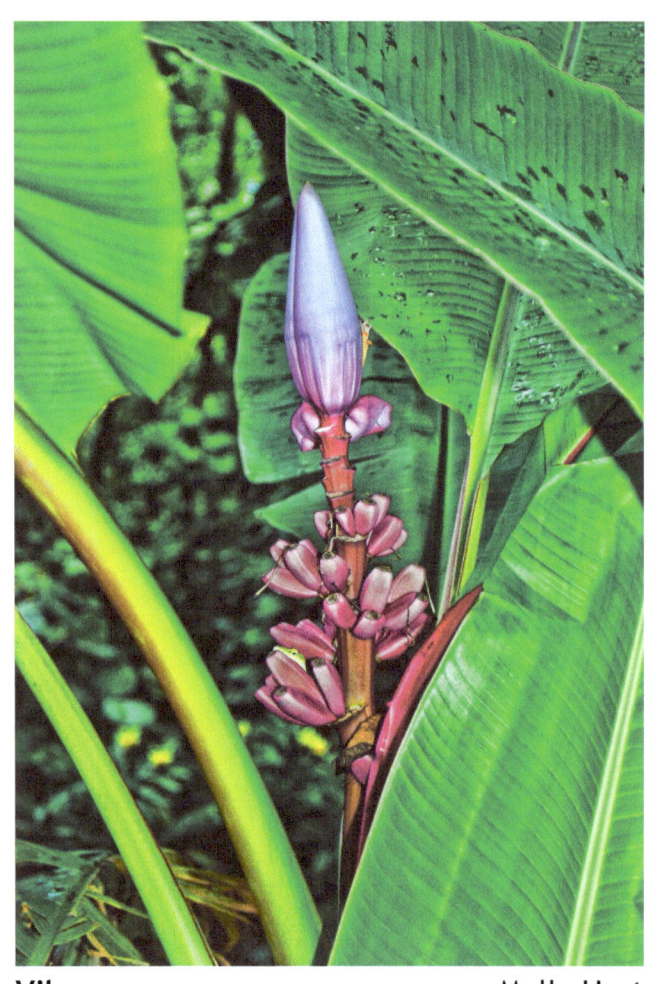

Vibrance Molly Hart

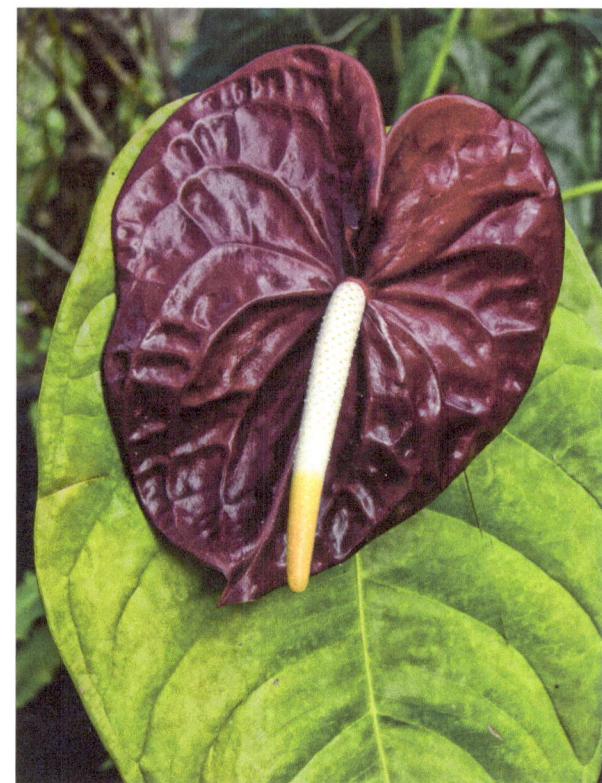

Anthurium Molly Hart

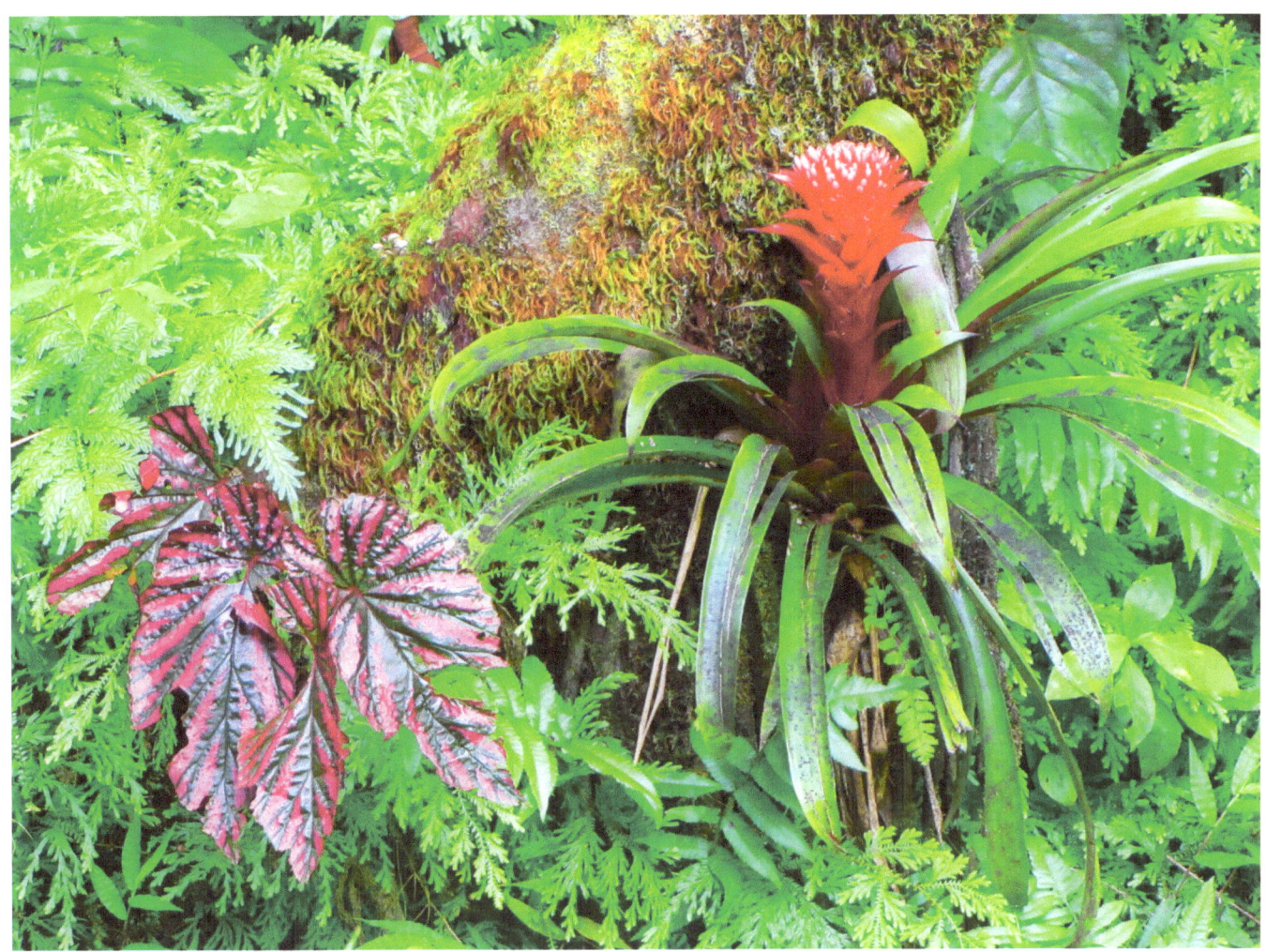

Verdant Balance   Kelly Hart

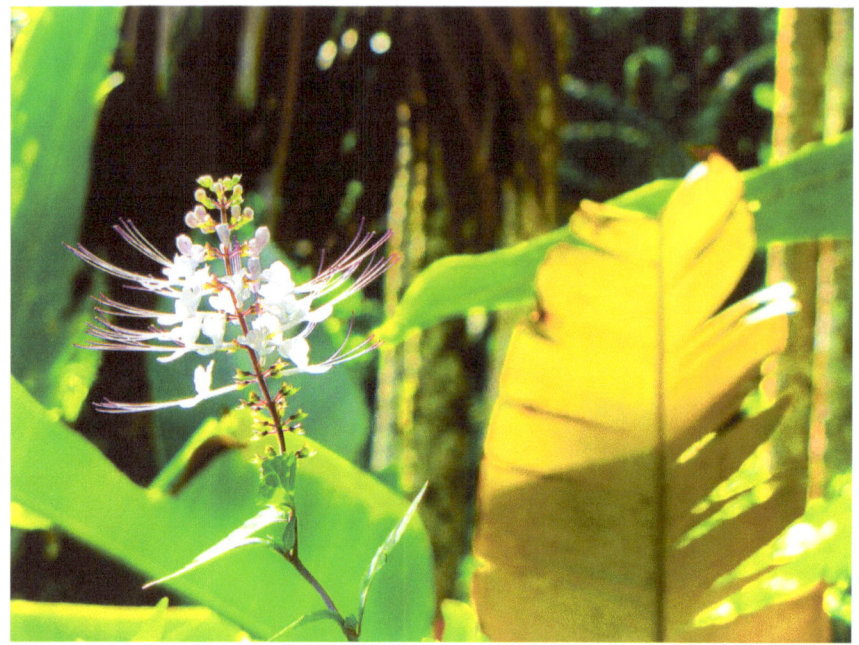

Wings of Light   Kelly Hart

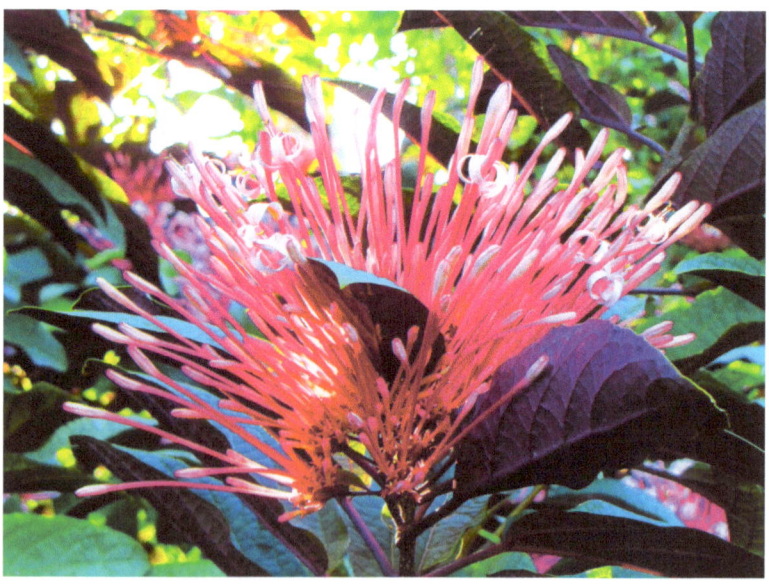

Colorful Explosion   Kelly Hart

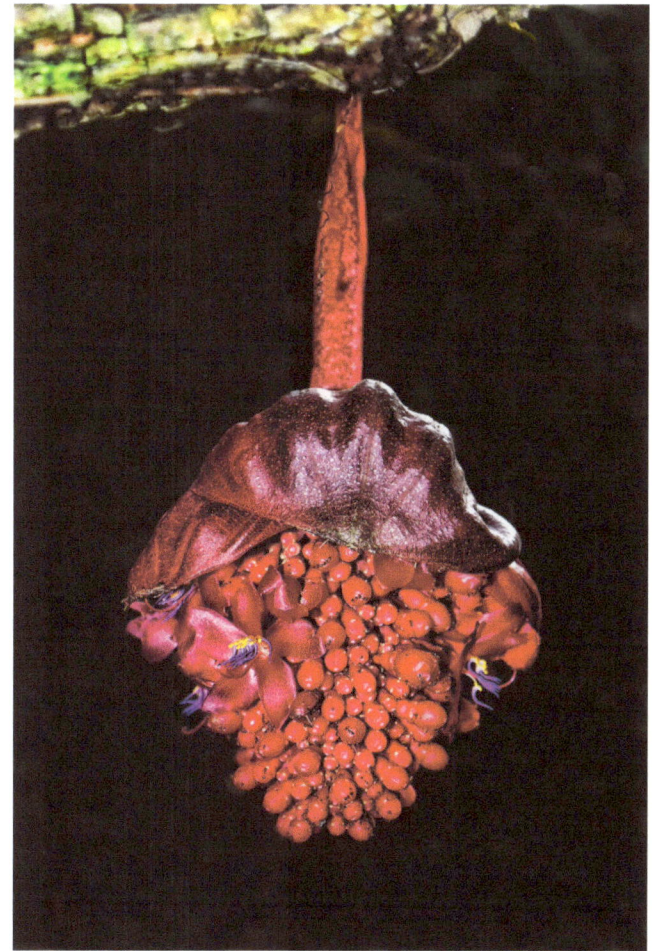

Heart of the Jungle   Molly Hart

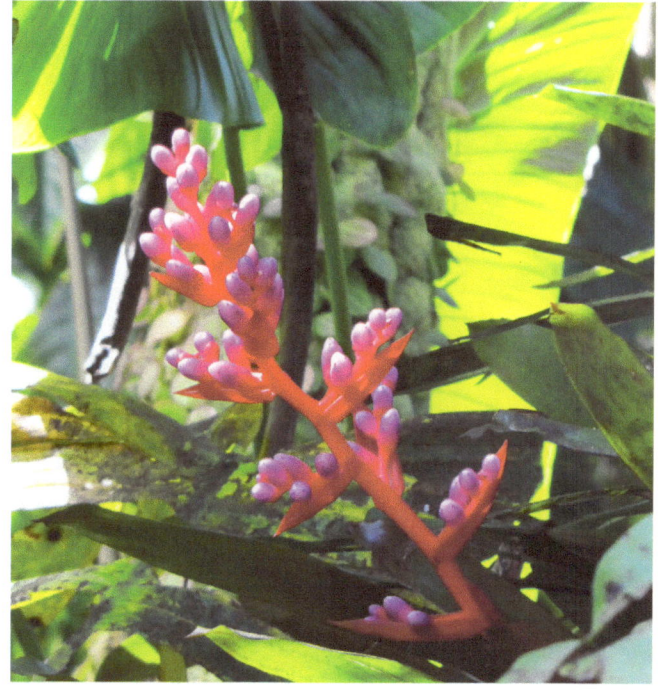

Chaotic Energy   Kelly Hart

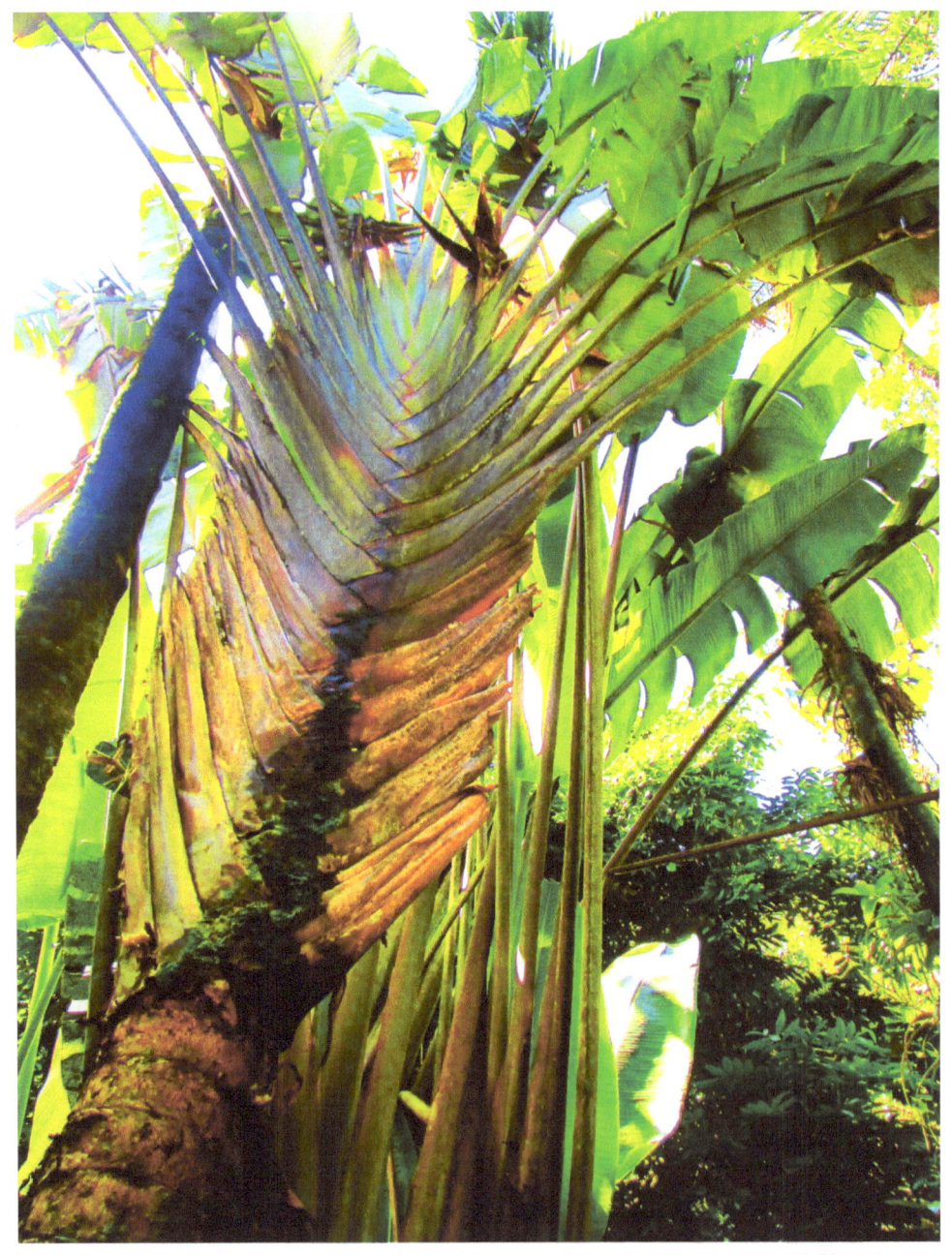

Woven Fan   Kelly Hart

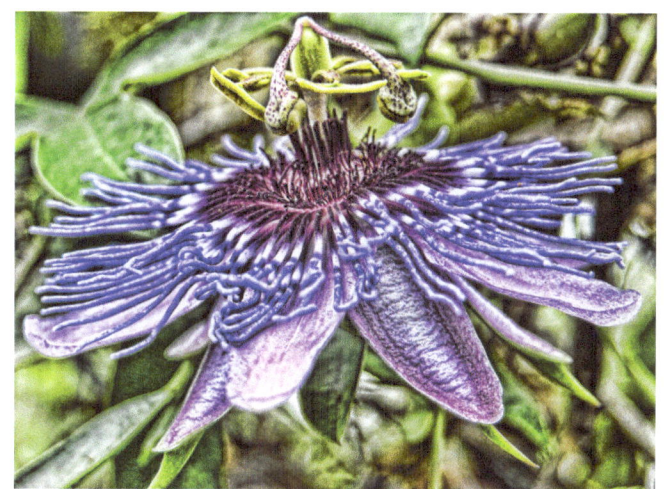

Passion Flower   Molly Hart

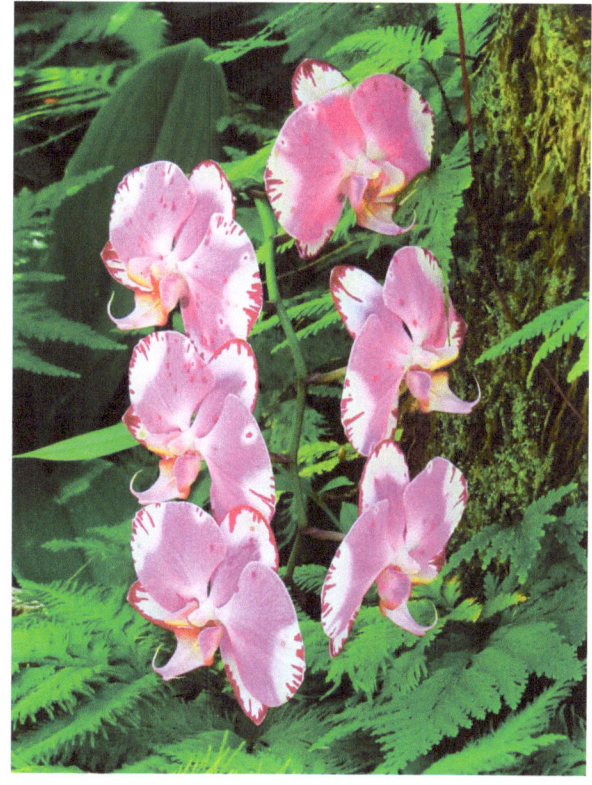

Orchid Dance   Kelly Hart

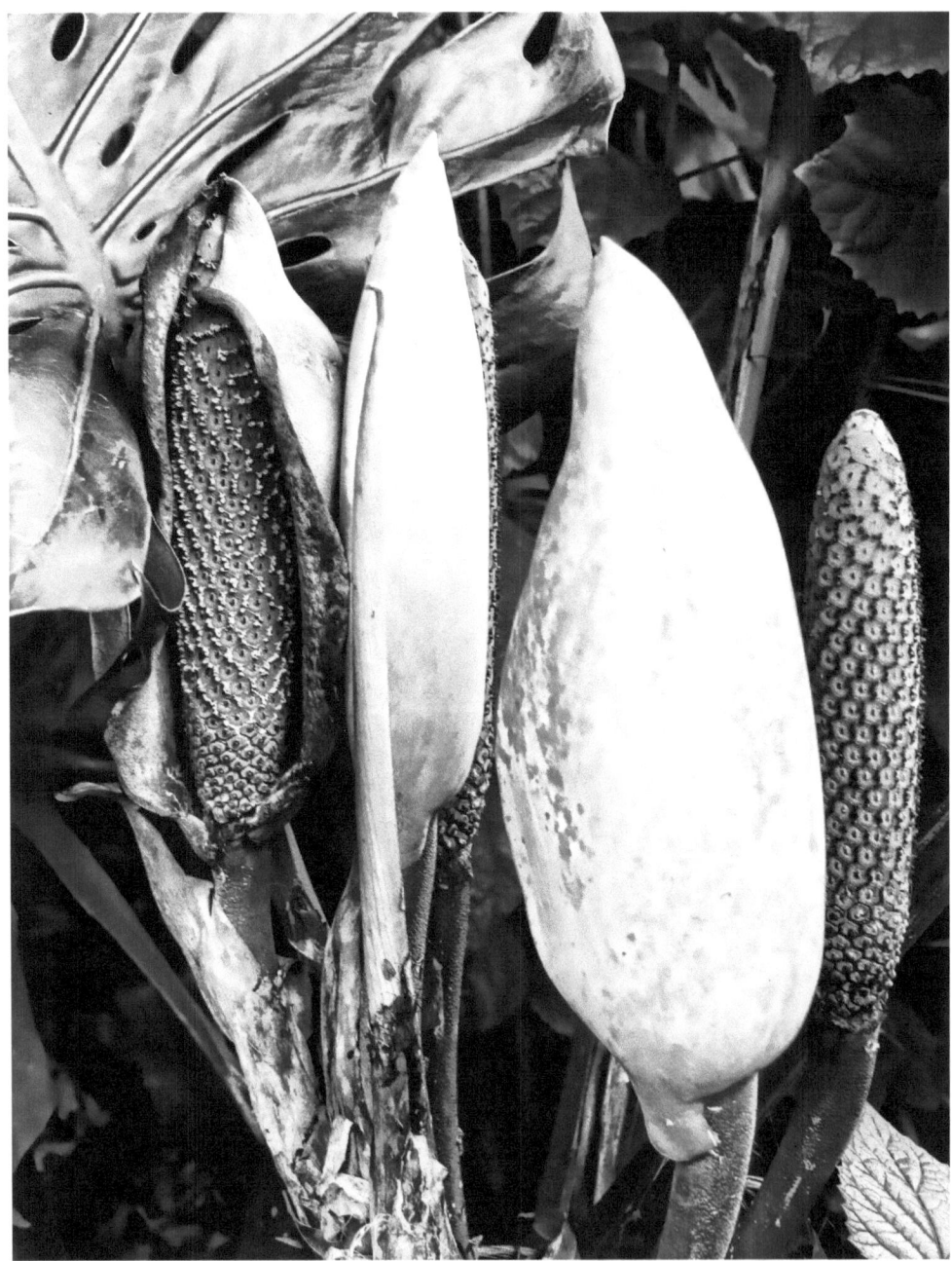

Moonlight Monstera   Molly Hart

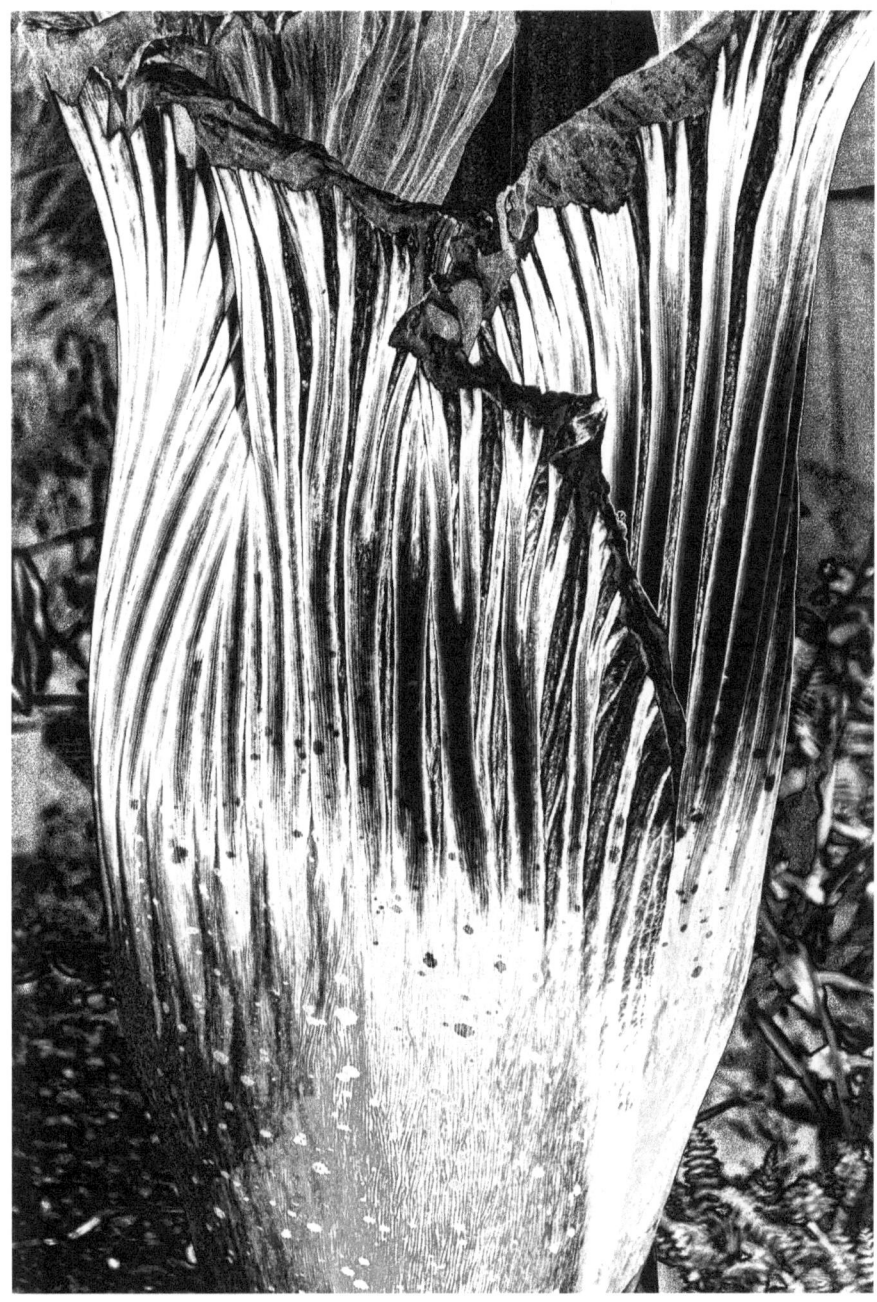

Stink Horn   Molly Hart

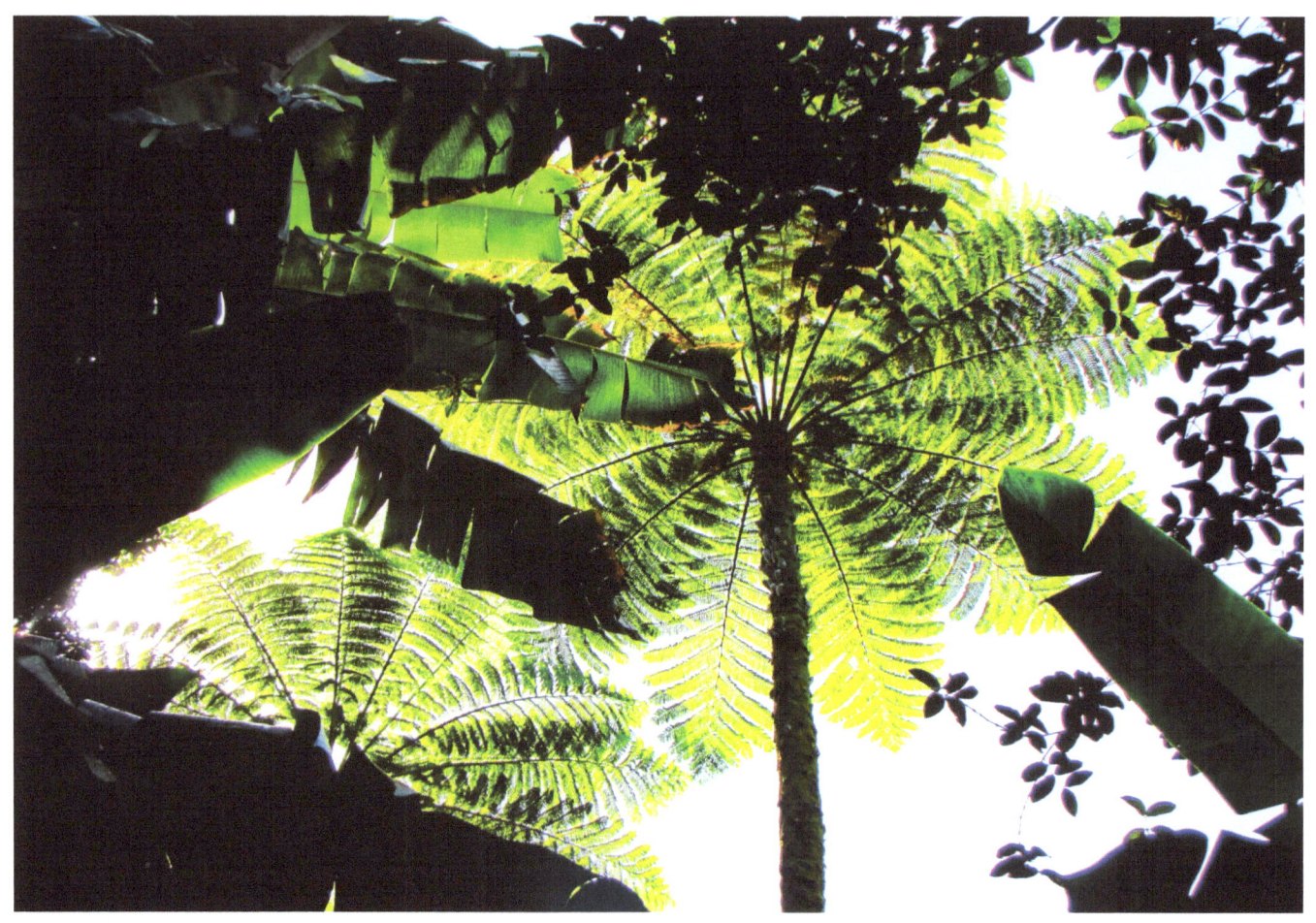

Whirling

Kelly Hart

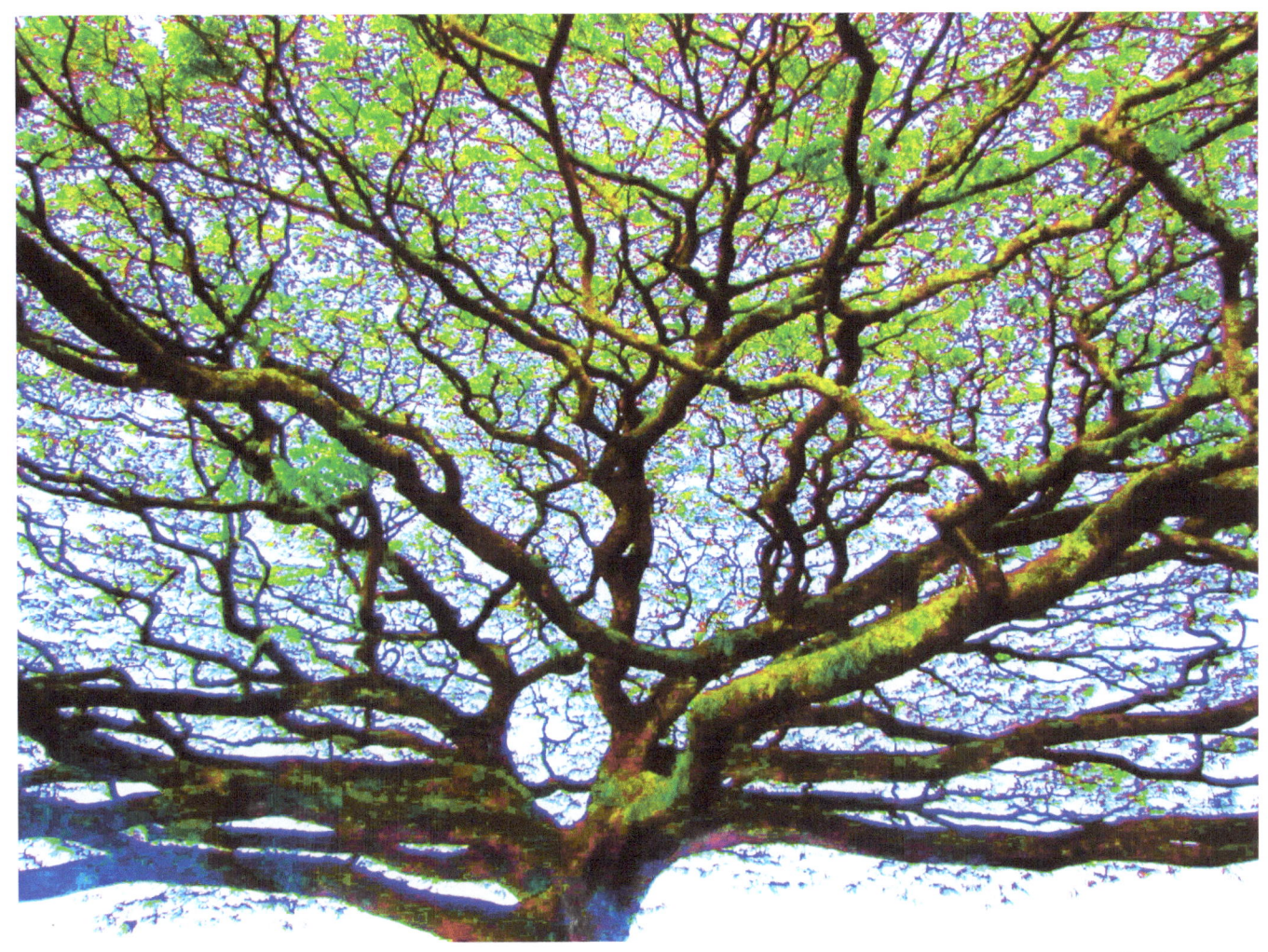

Good Vibes

Kelly Hart

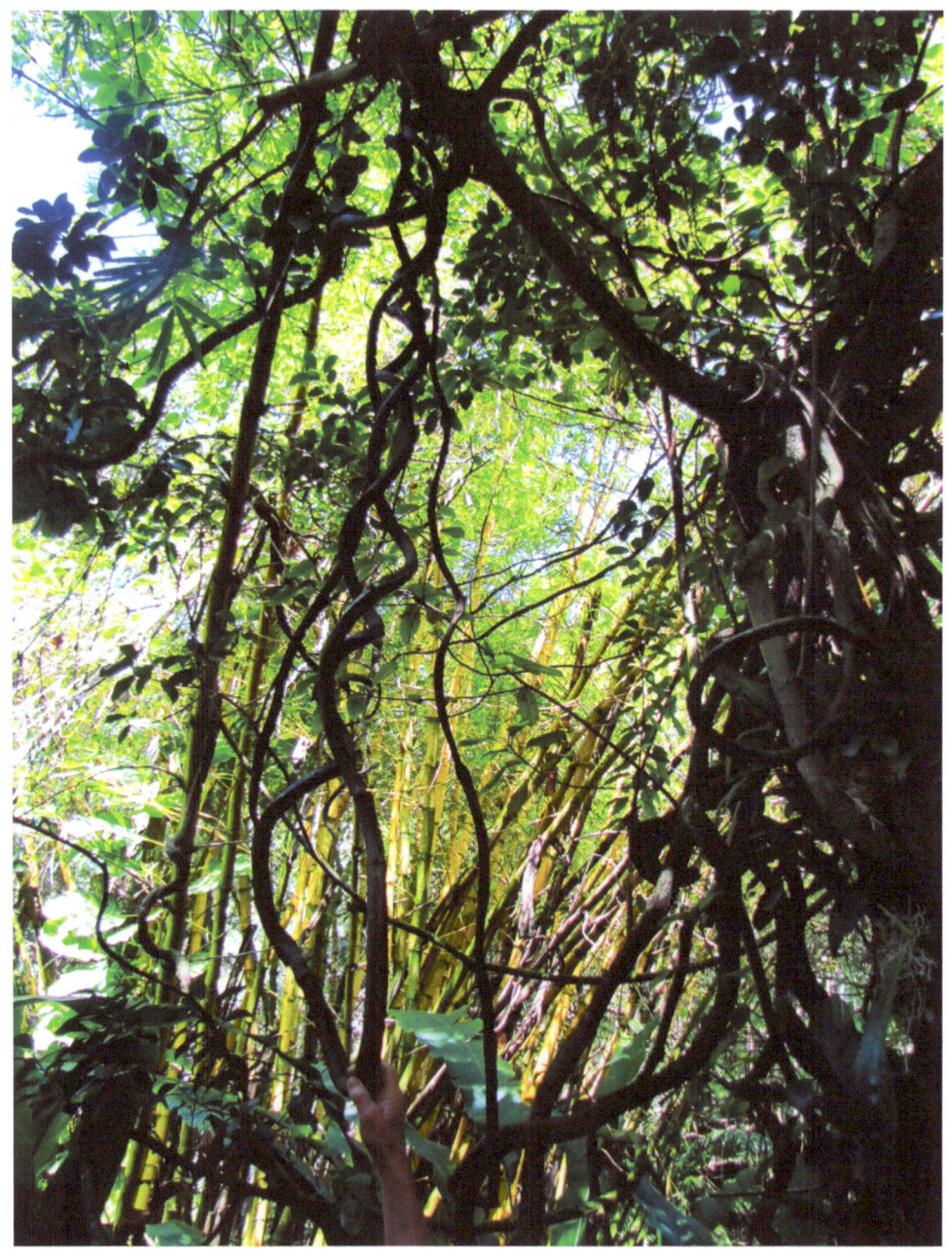

Reaching Vines   Kelly Hart

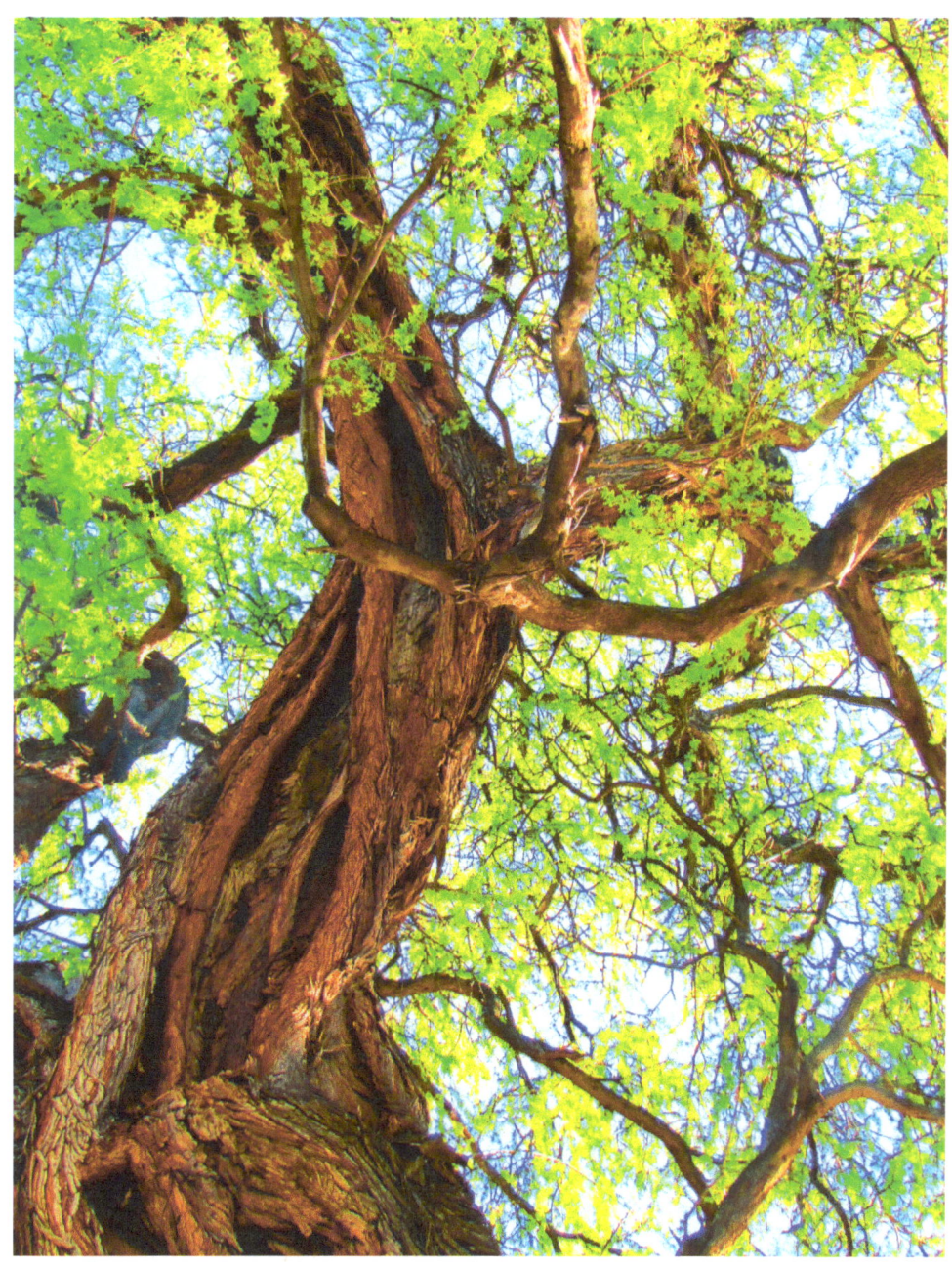

Twisted Dance   Kelly Hart

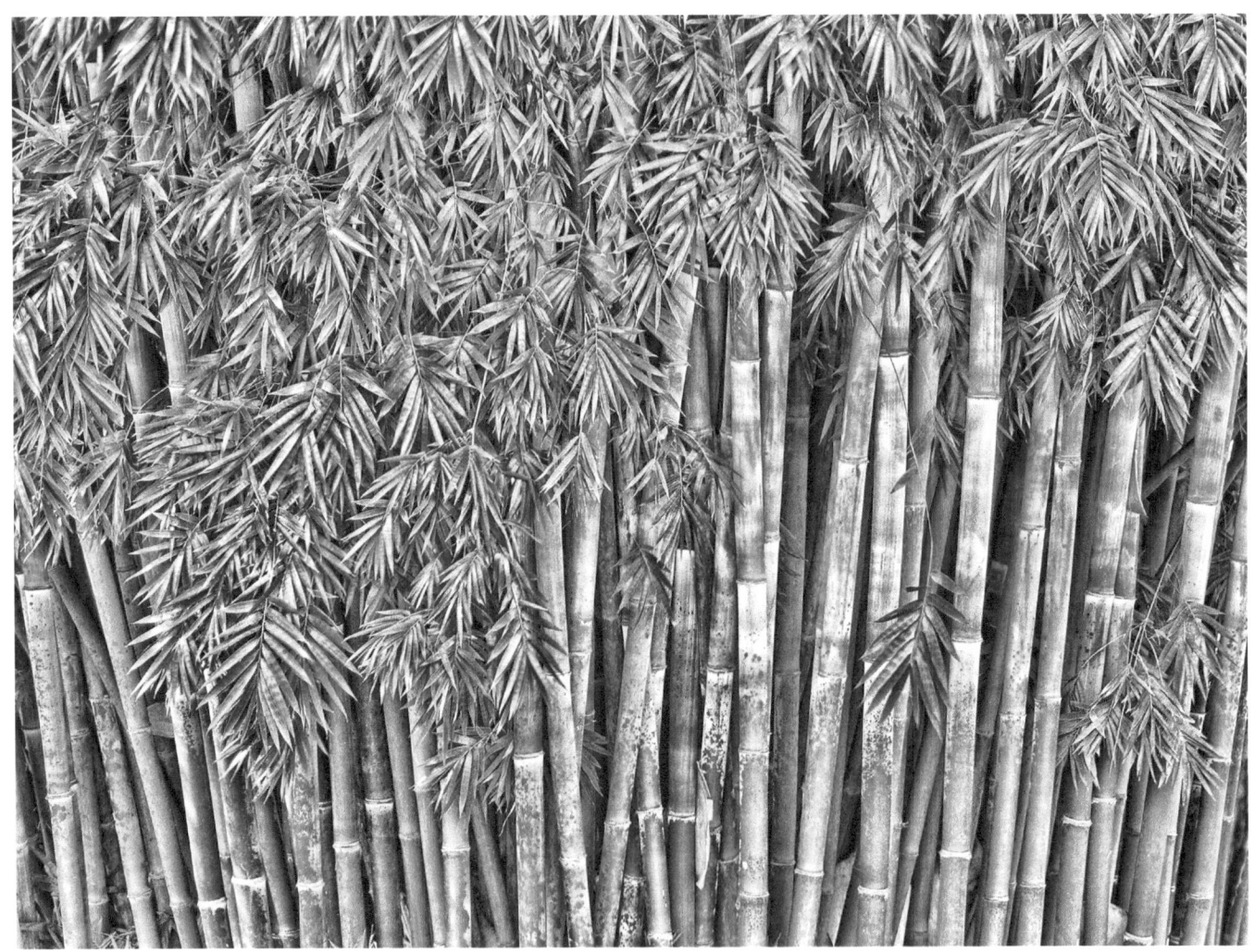

Magical Forest

Molly Hart

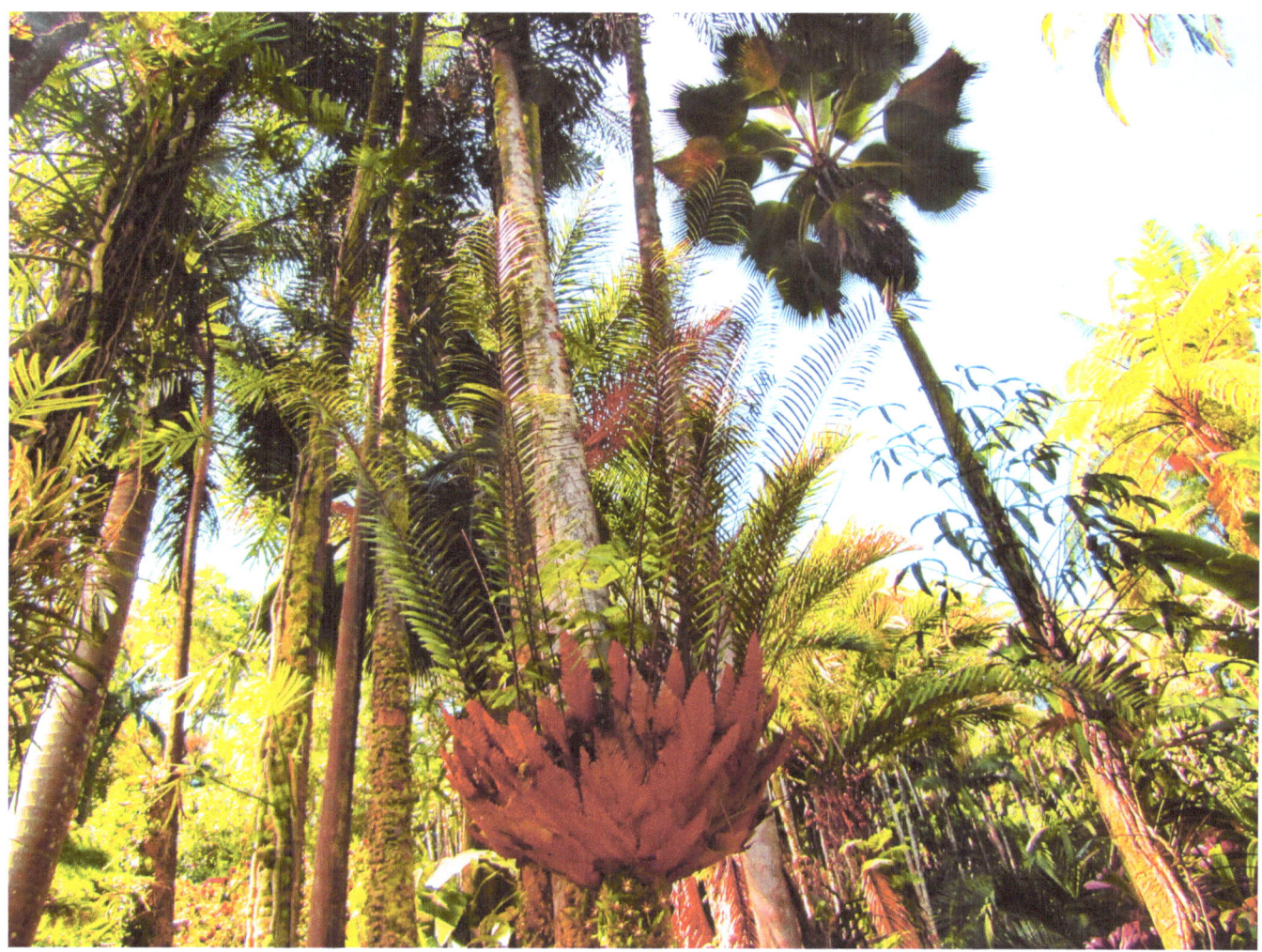

Culmination

Kelly Hart

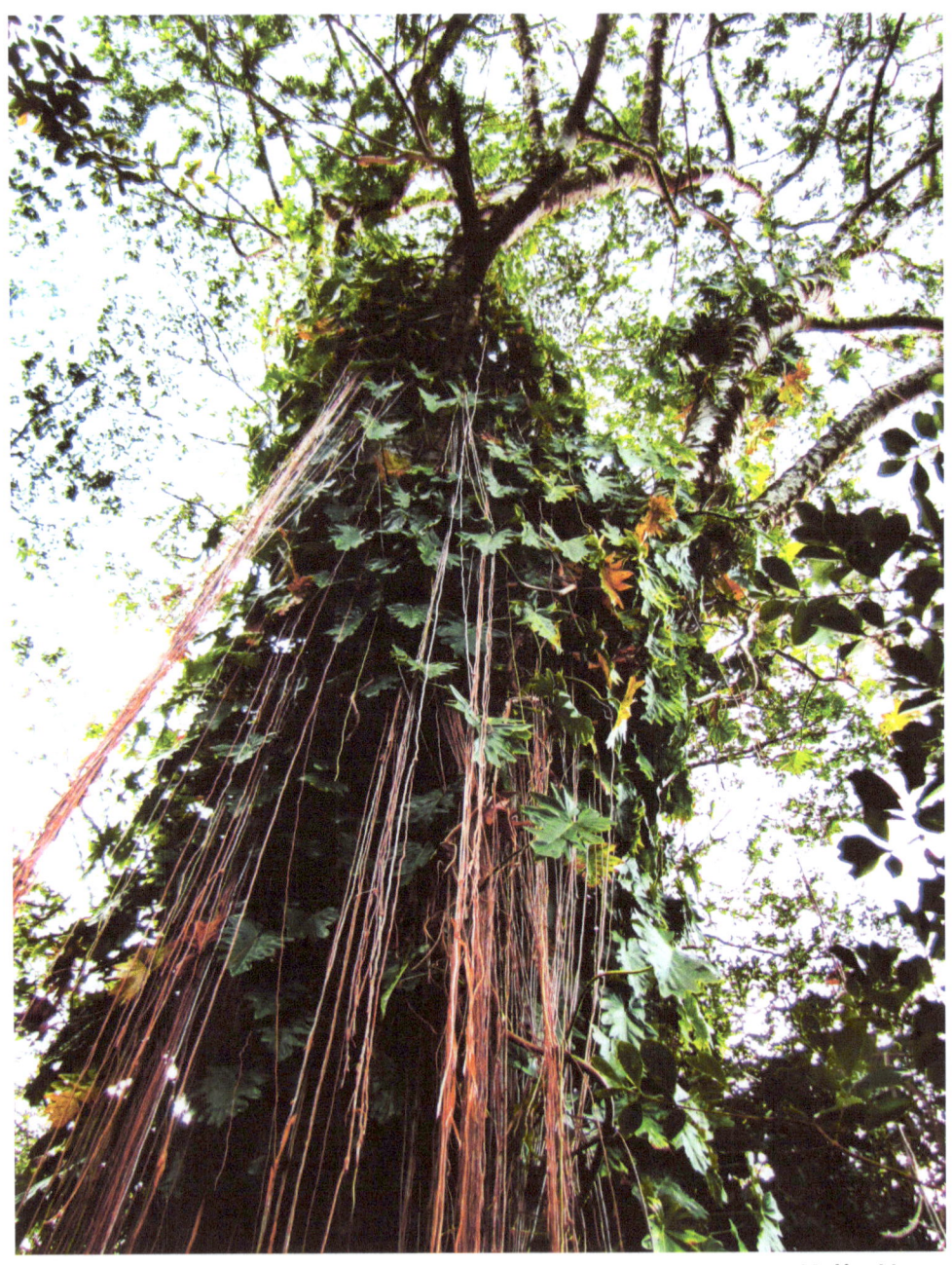

Tendrils   Kelly Hart

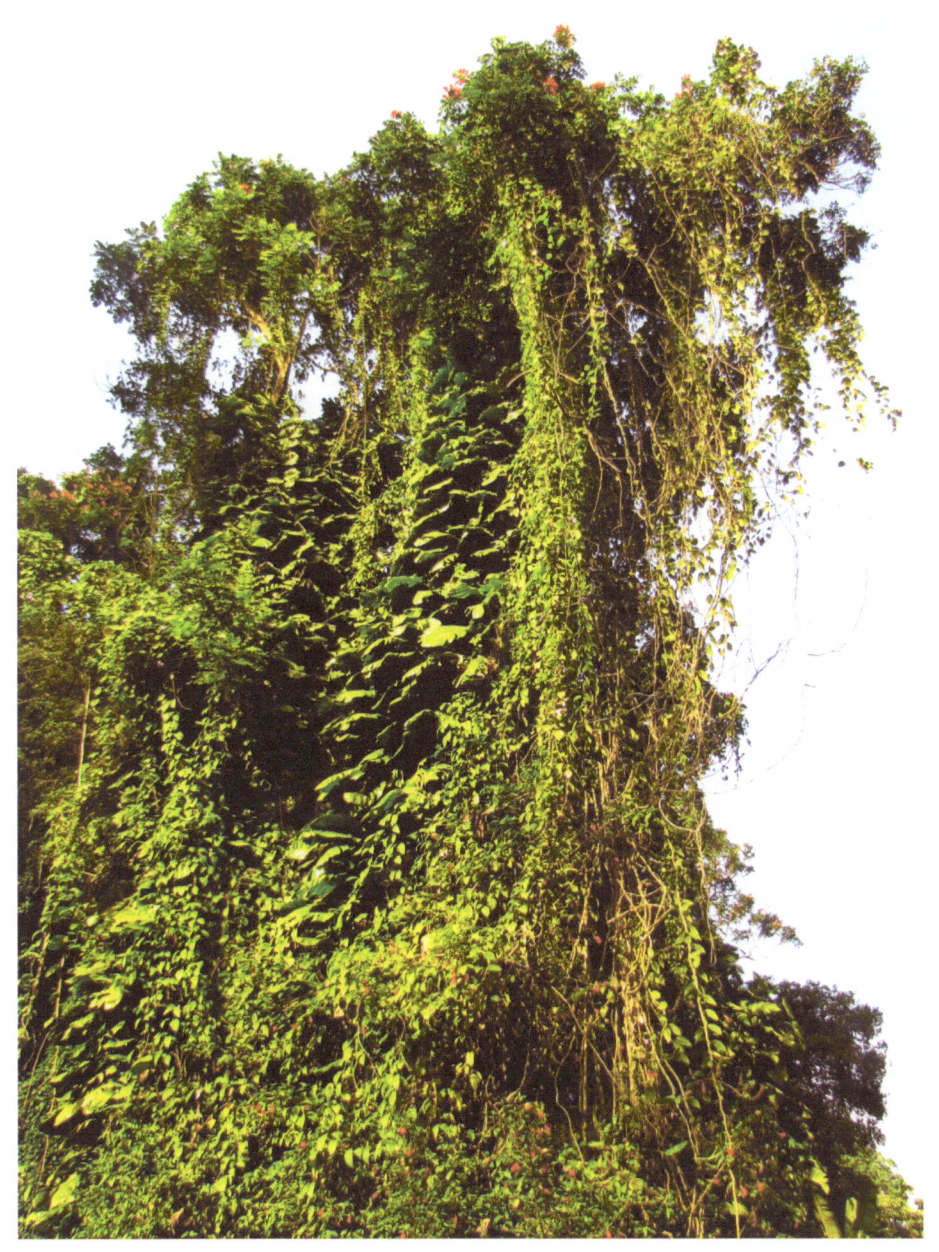

Vining to Heaven   Kelly Hart

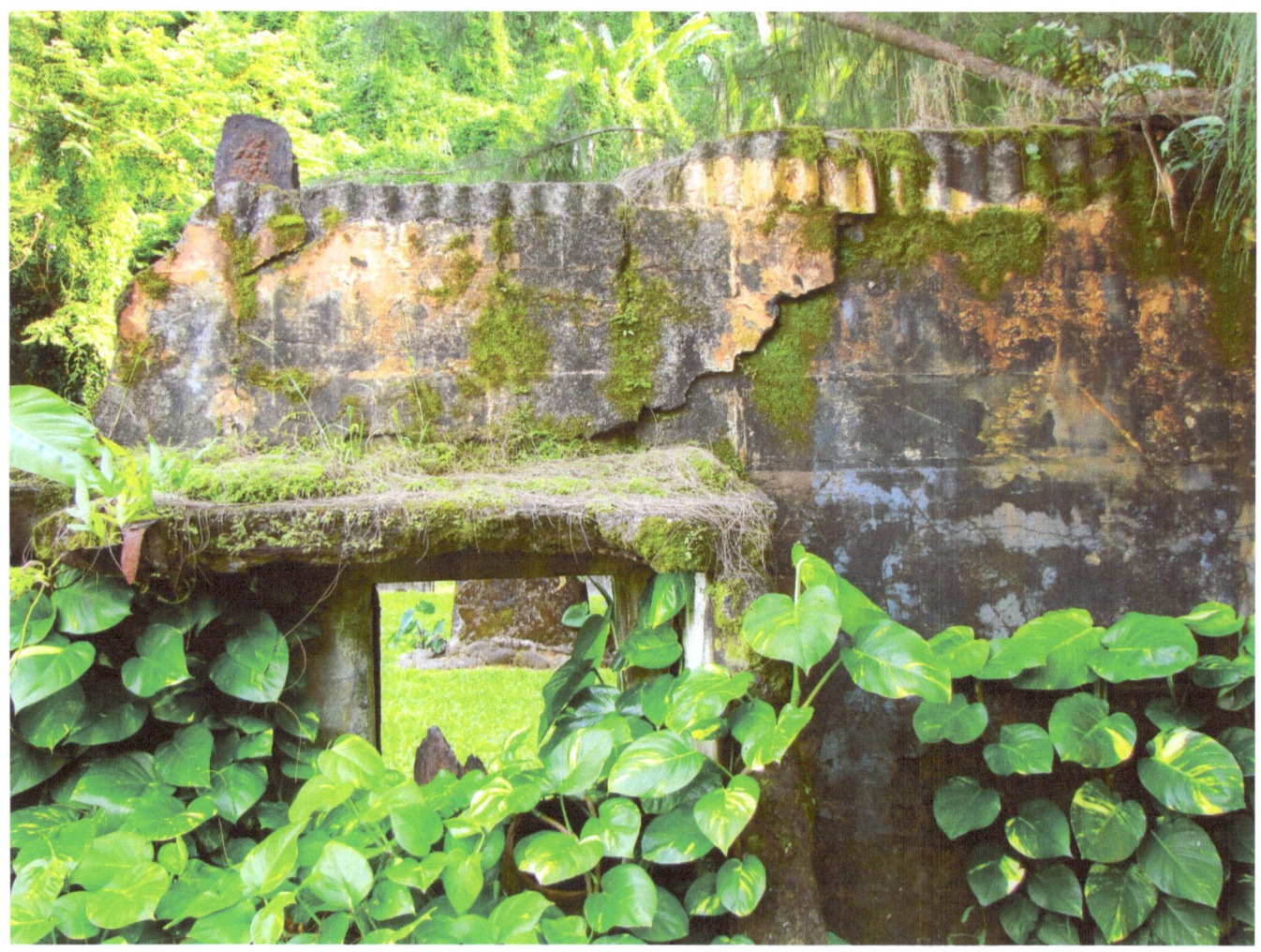

Ruins

Kelly Hart

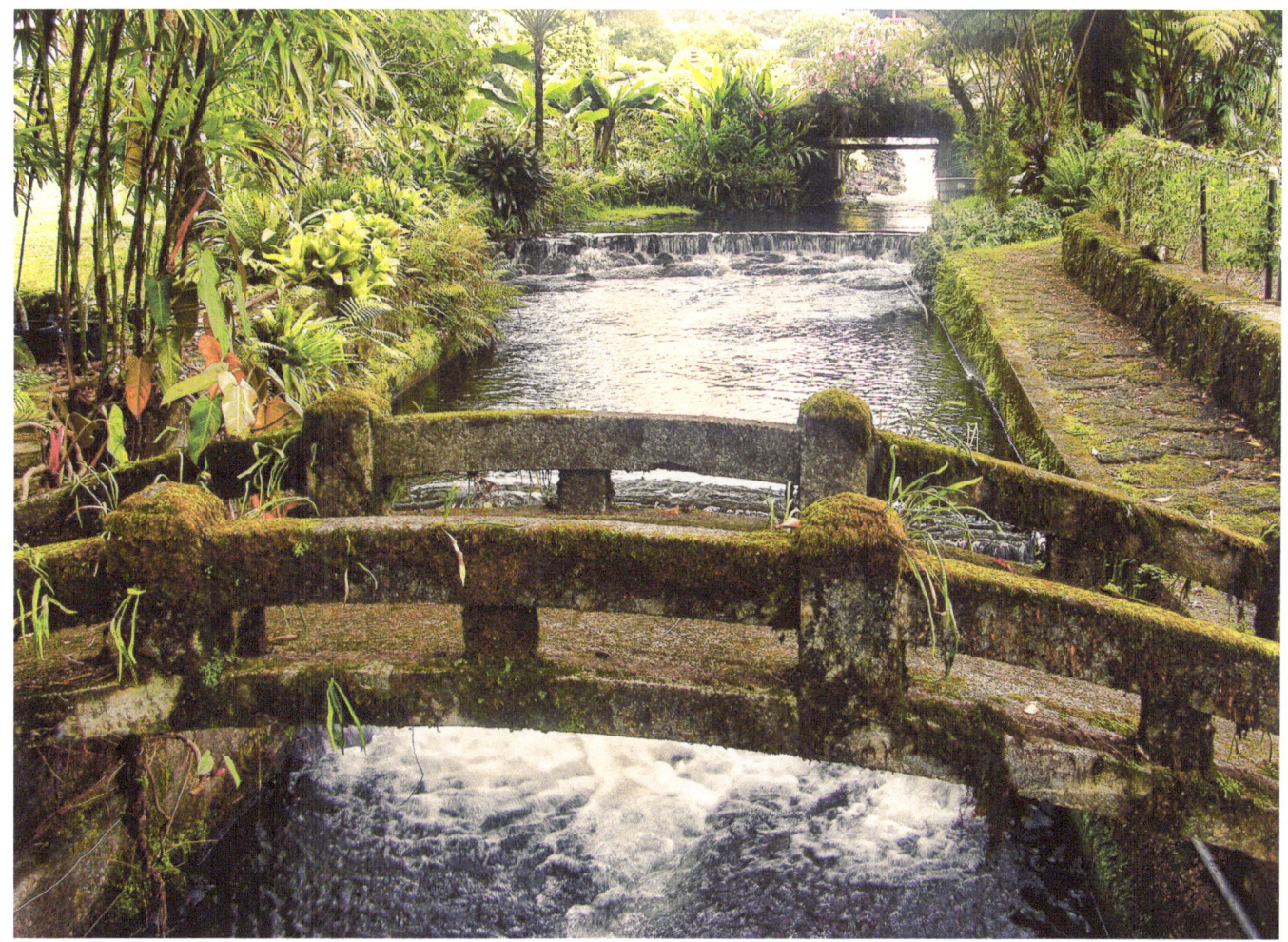

Mossy Bridge

Molly Hart

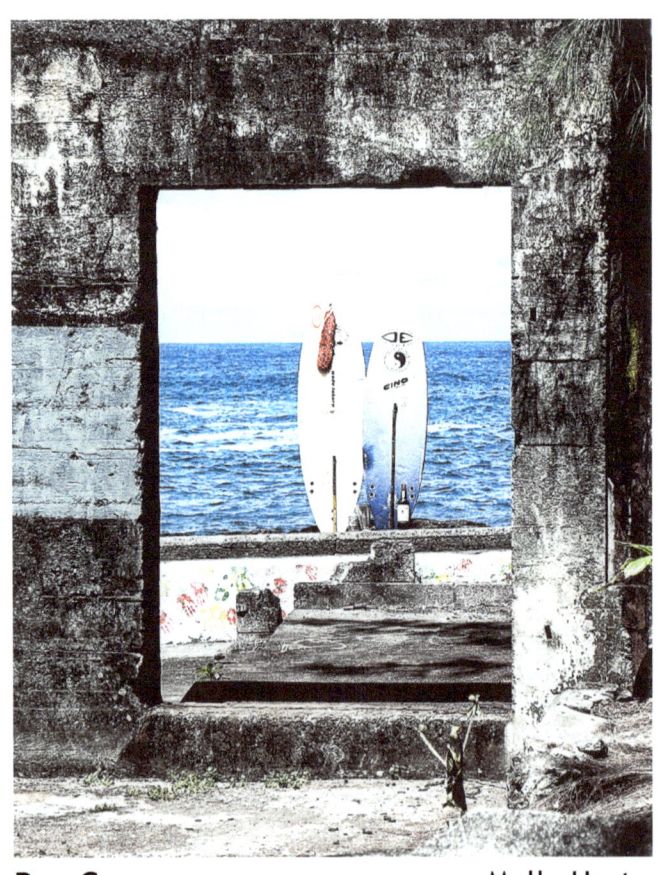

Bye Gone   Molly Hart

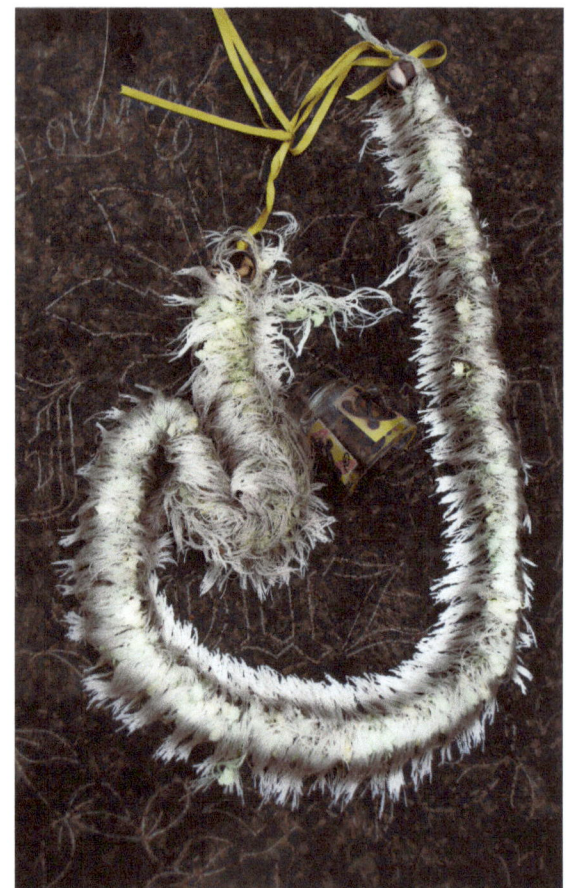

Last Lei   Molly Hart

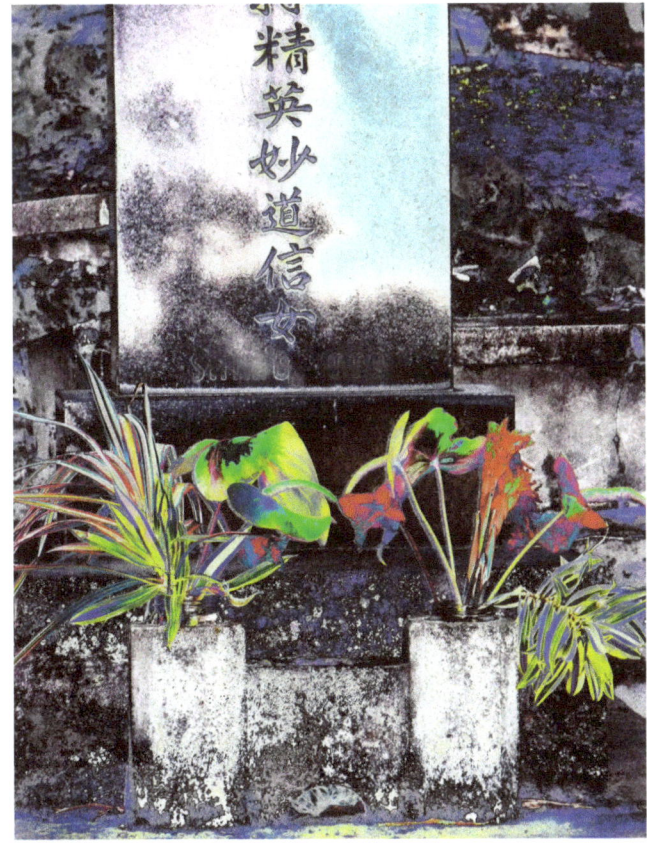

Ode to Ota Molly Hart

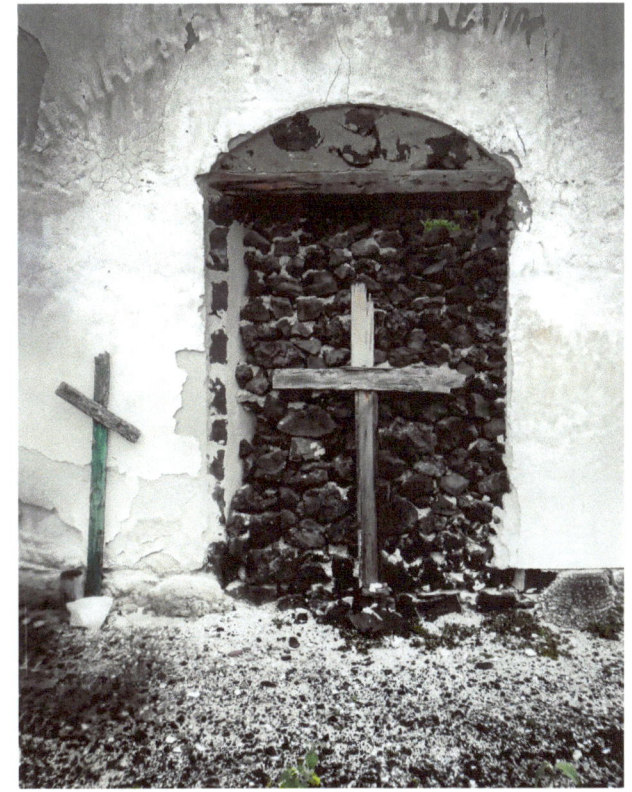

Double Crossed Molly Hart

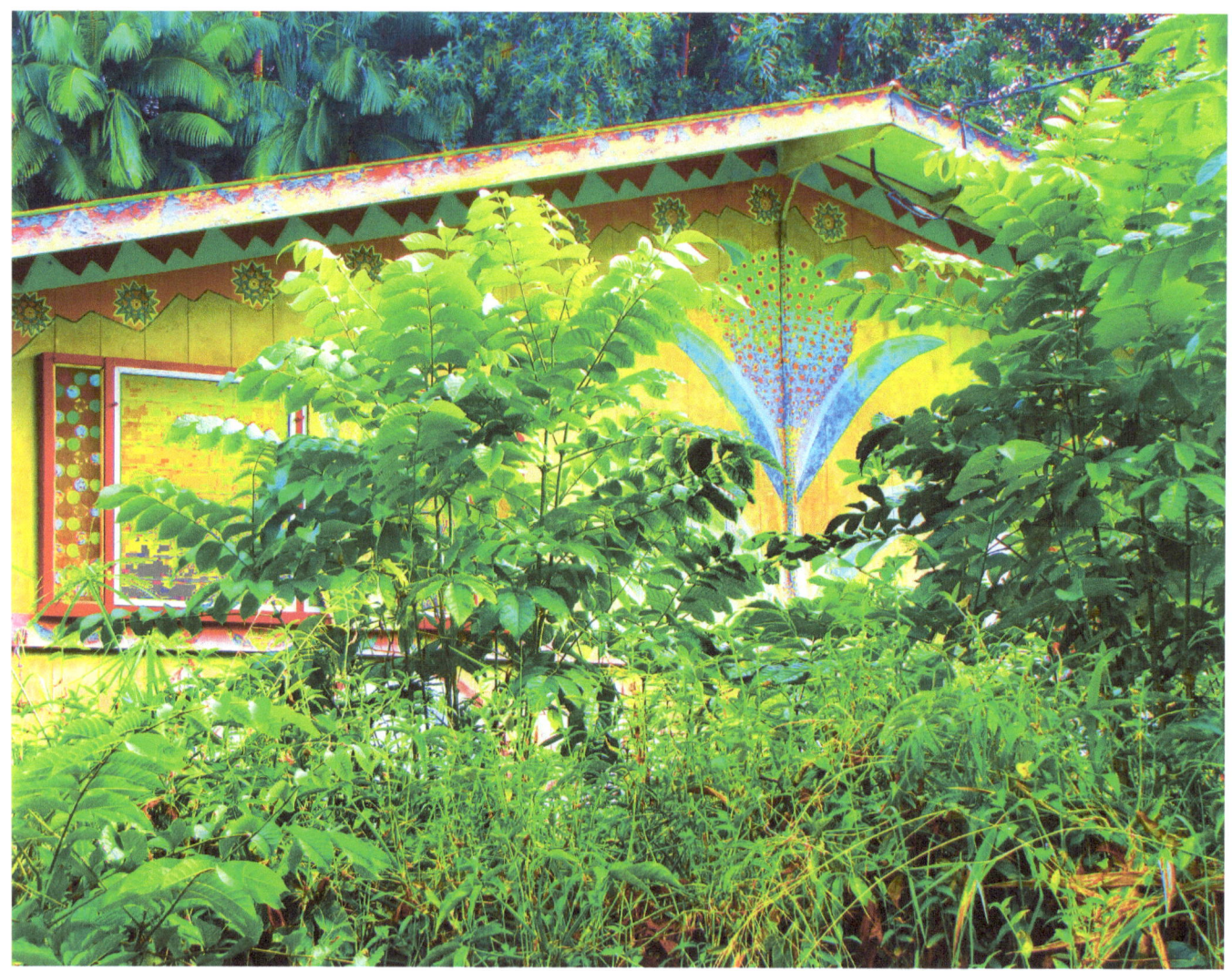

Past Glory

Kelly Hart

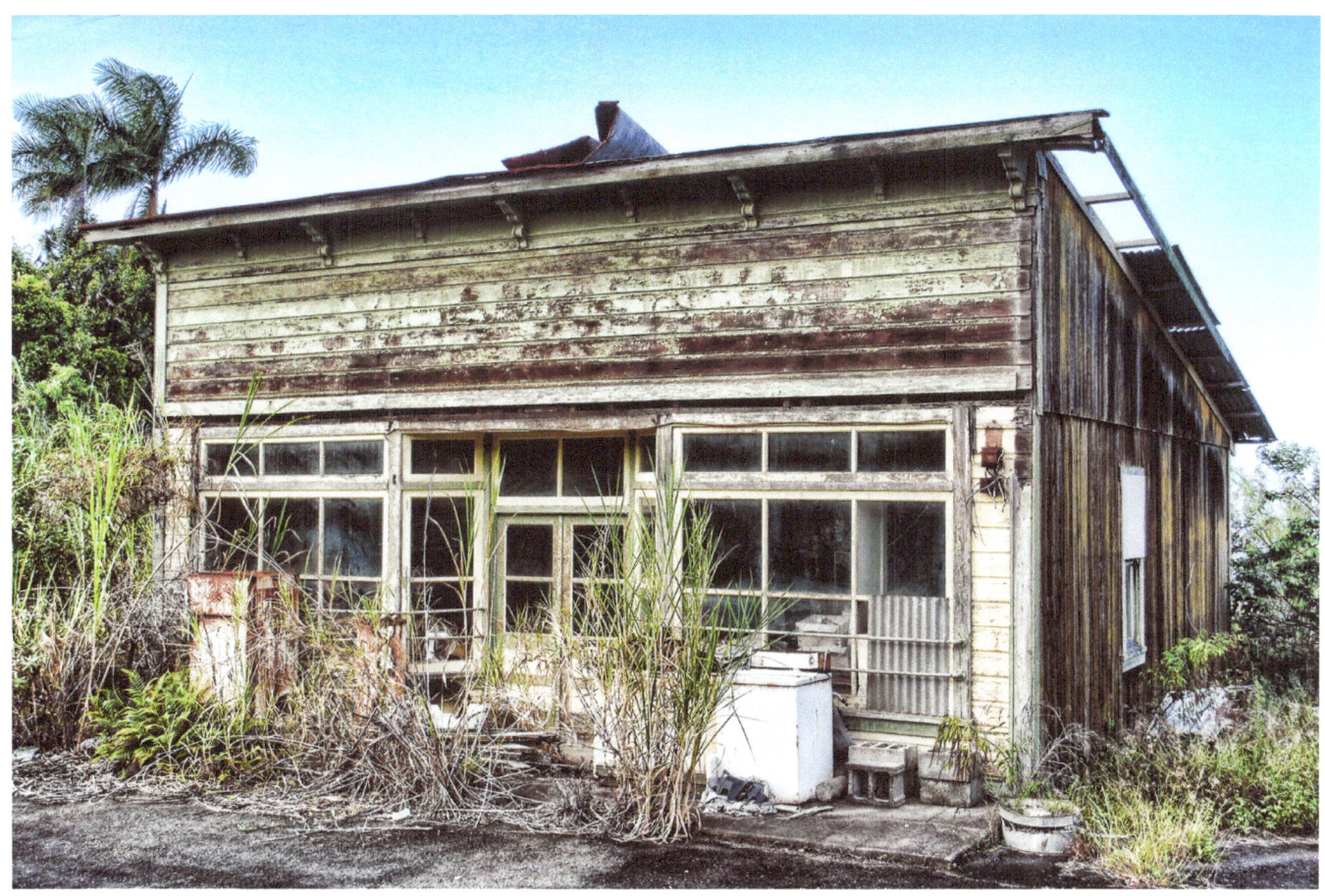

Dry Goods   Molly Hart

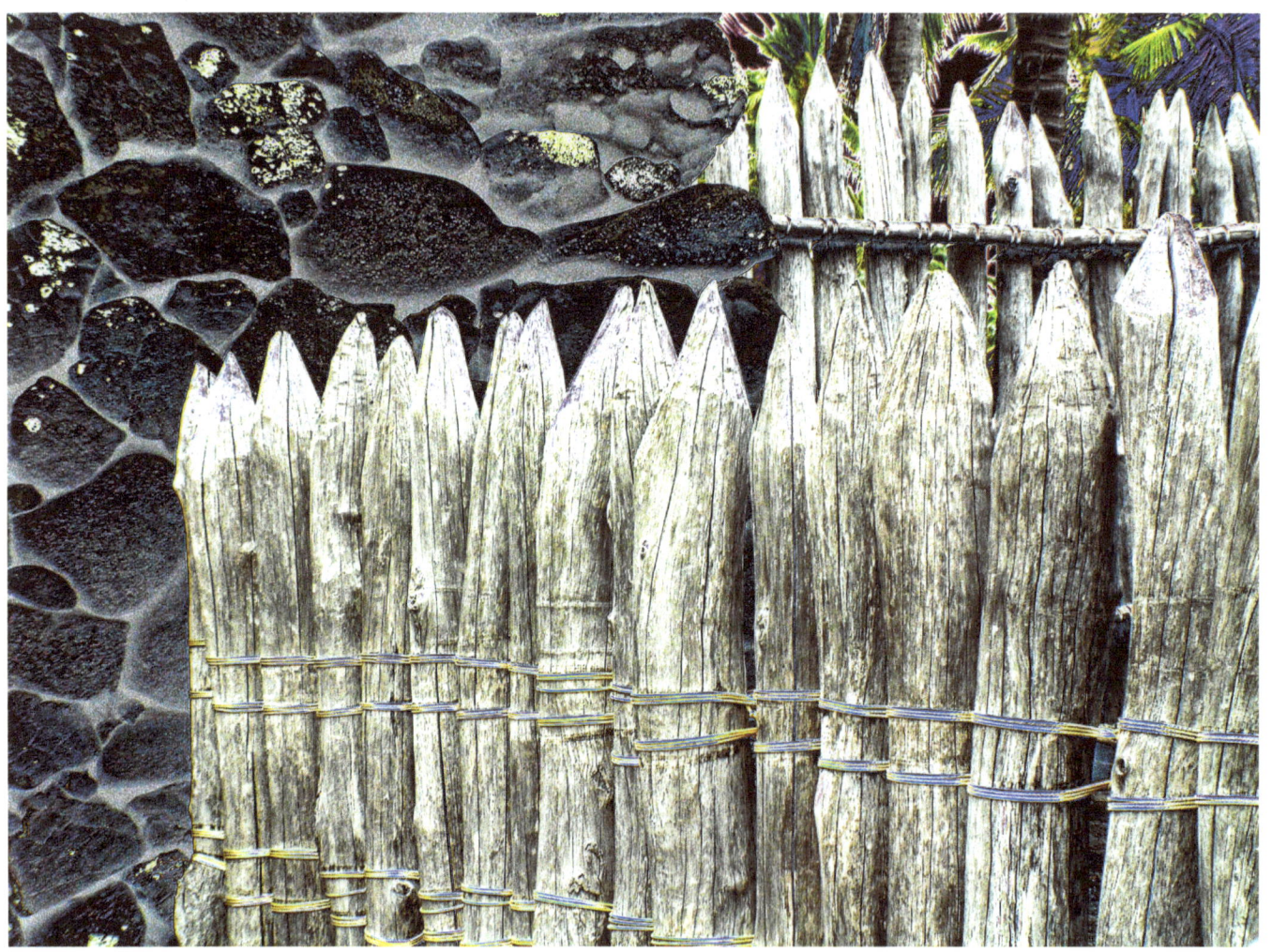

Pu'uhonua O Honaunau   Molly Hart

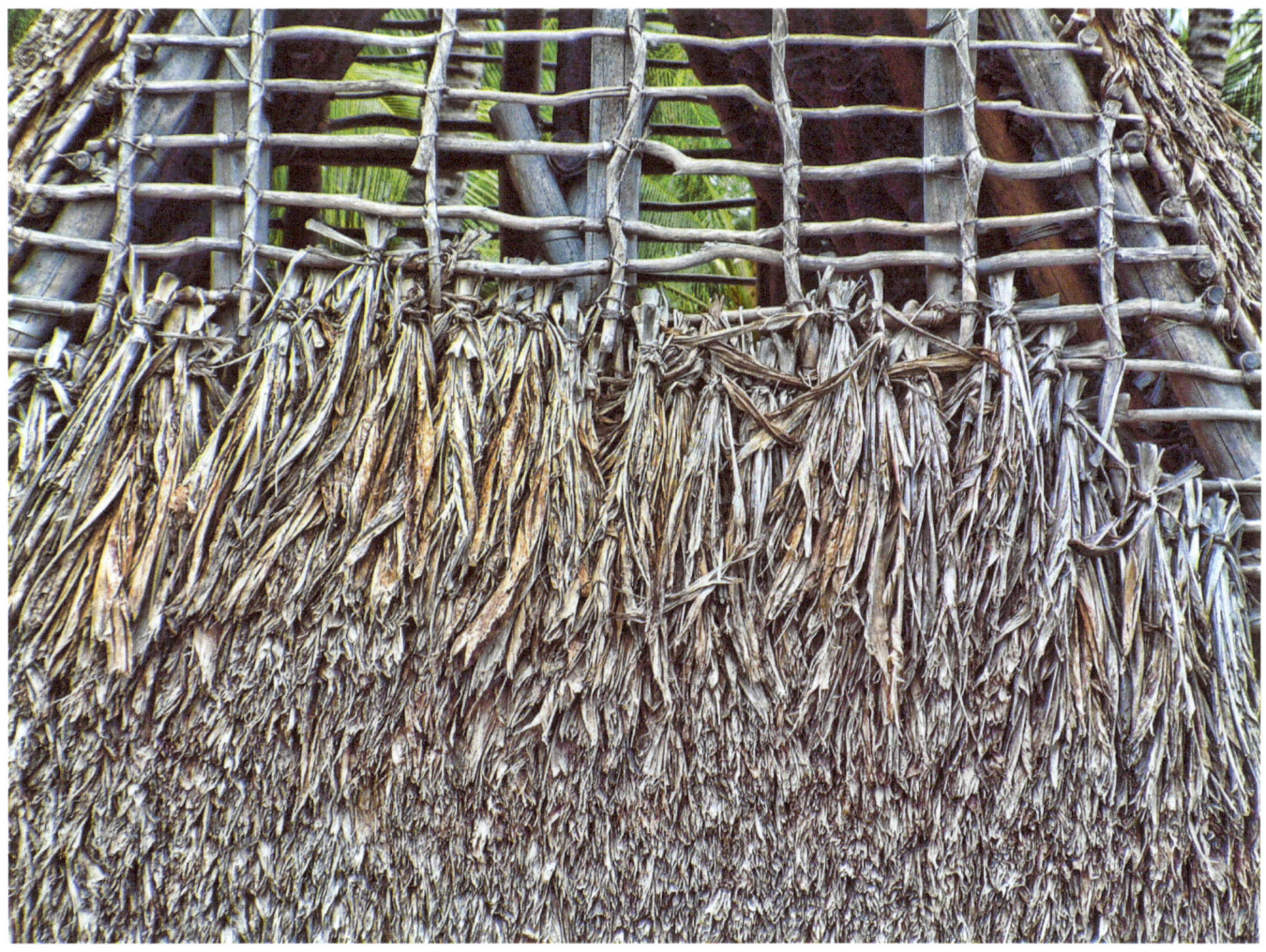

Thatching Molly Hart

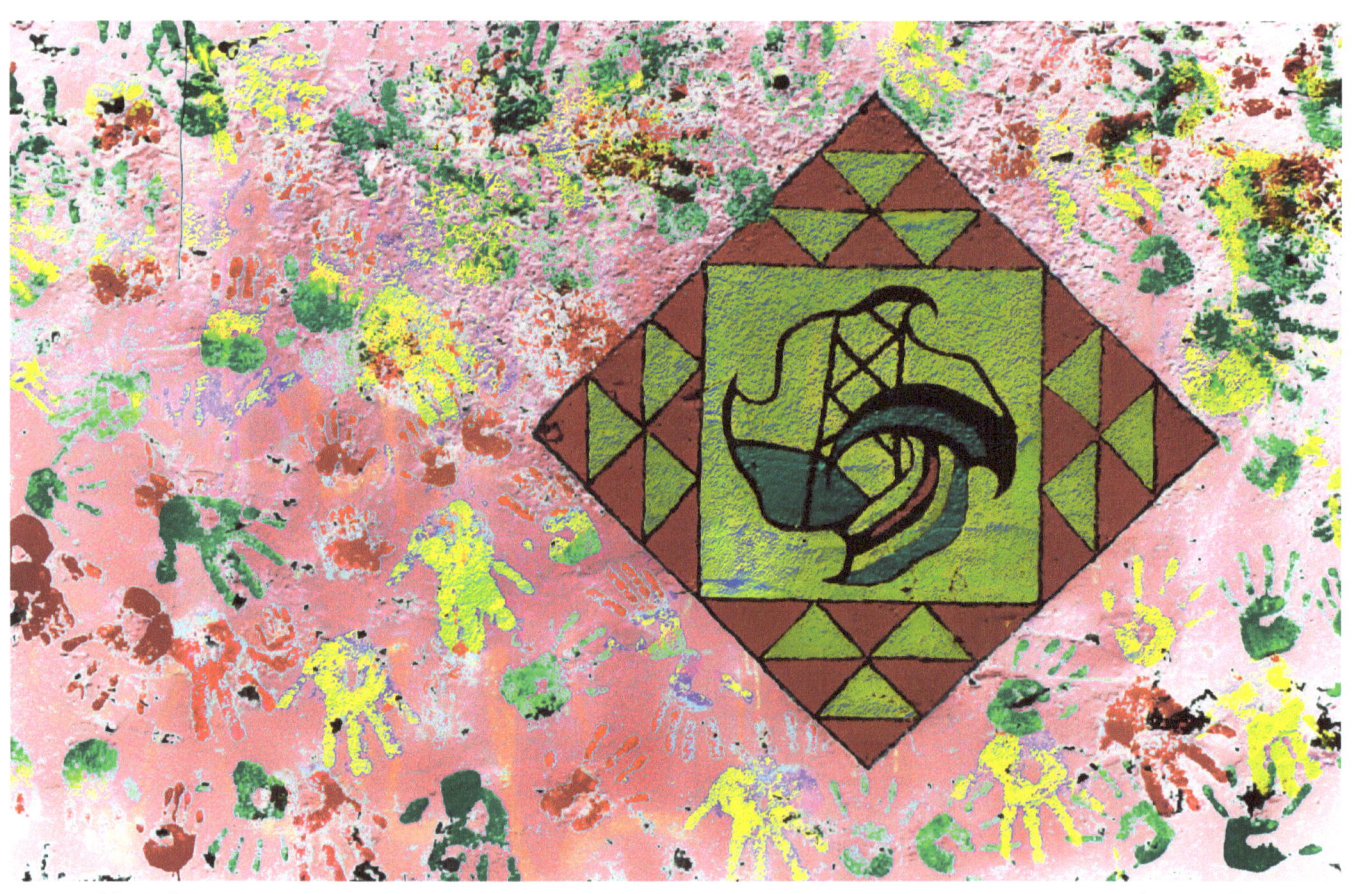

Many Hands

Molly Hart

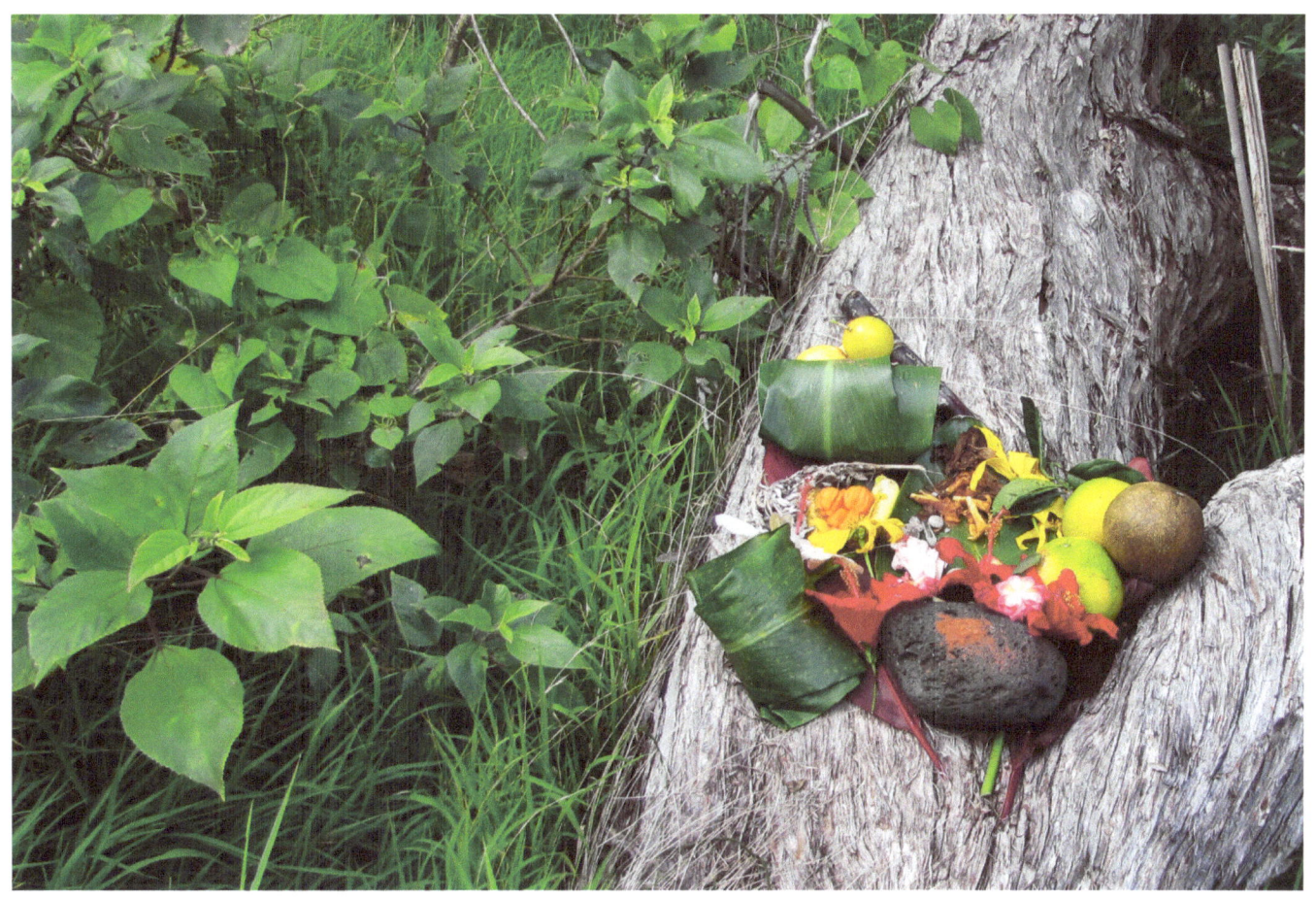

Offering   Kelly Hart

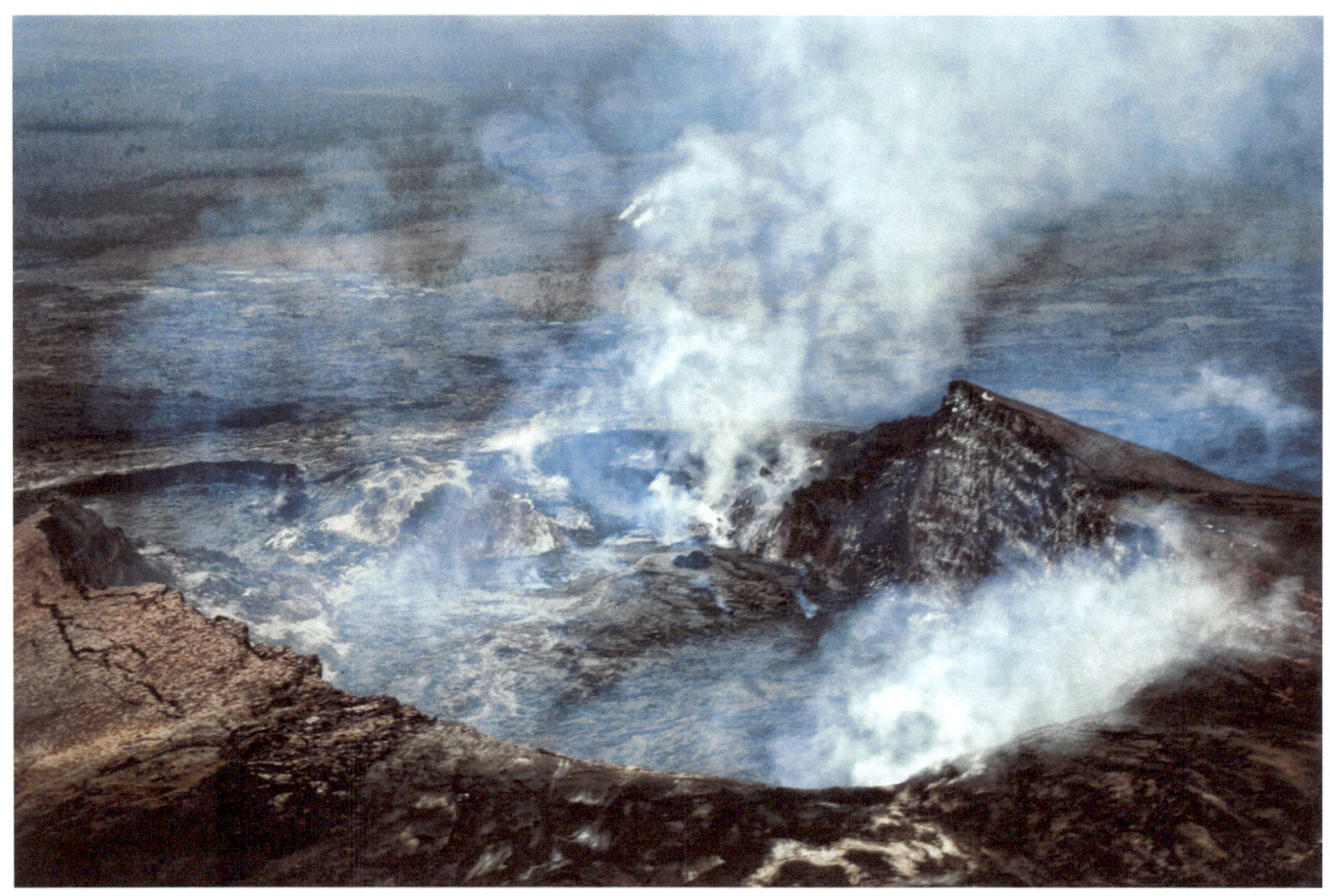

Caldera

Molly Hart

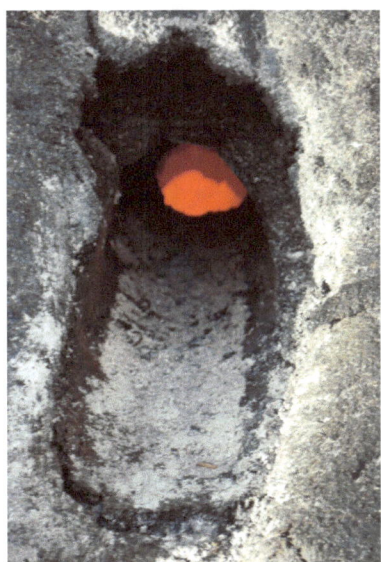

Fire in the Hole Molly Hart

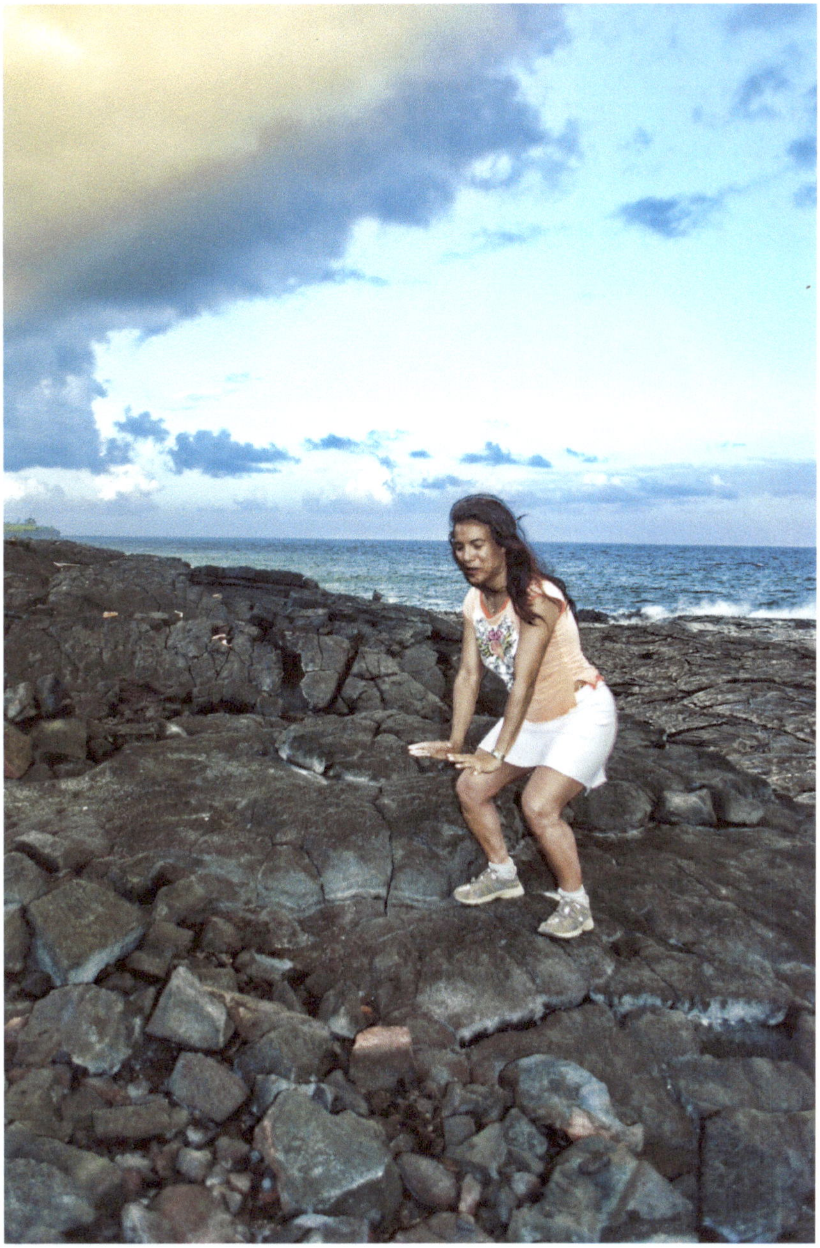

Karesa Pele Dance   Molly Hart

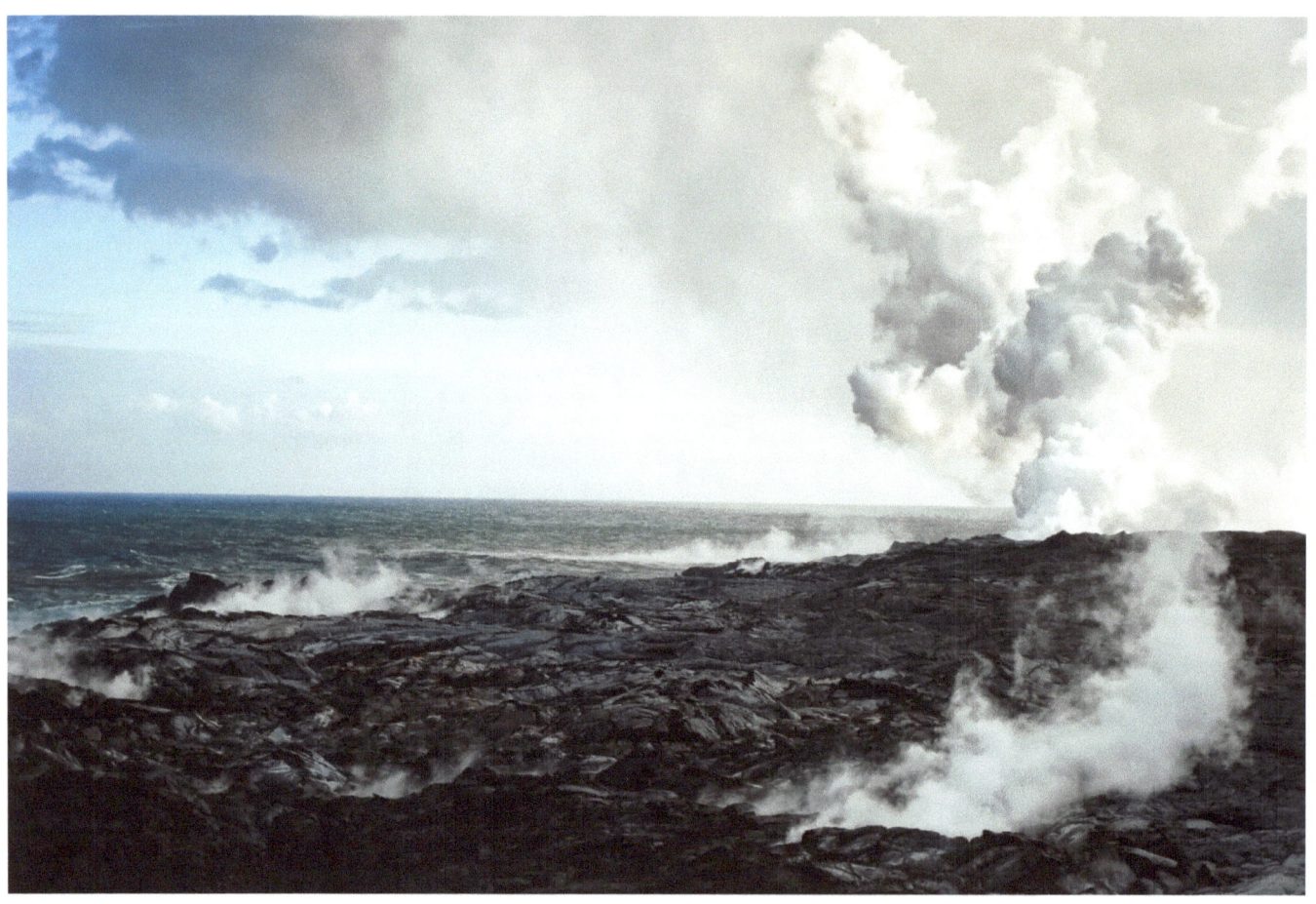

Plume

Molly Hart

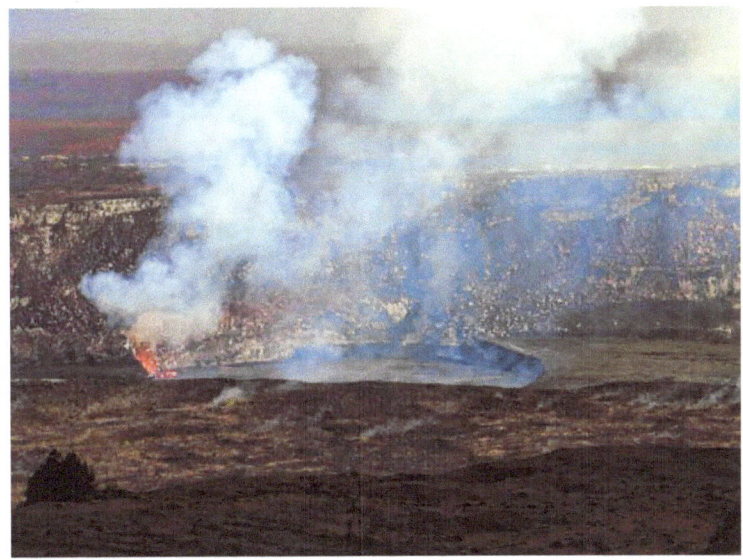

Lava Lake   Molly Hart

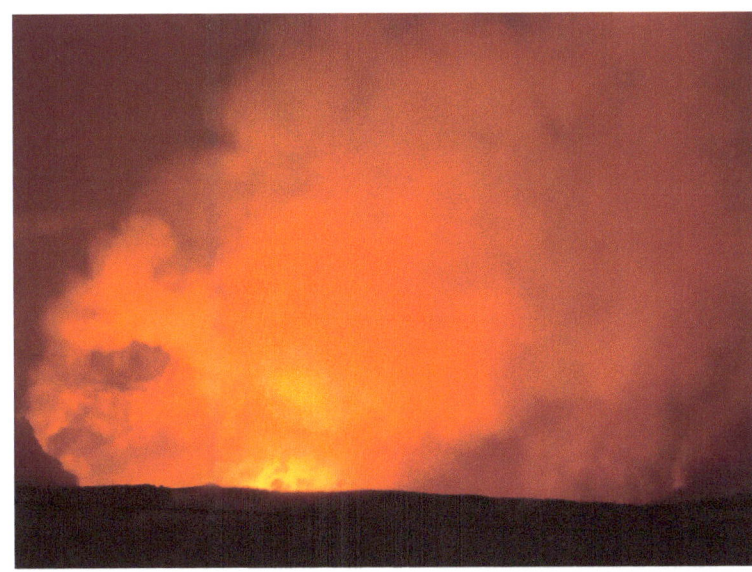

Fire and Brimstone   Kelly Hart

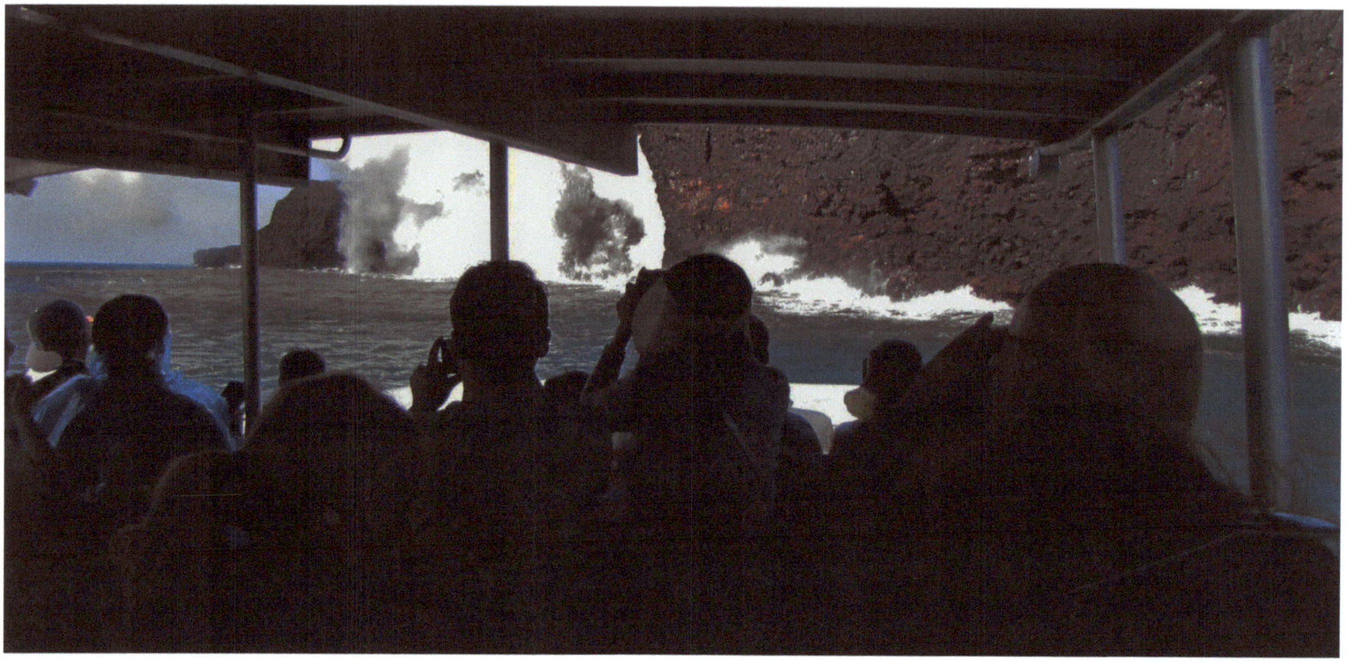

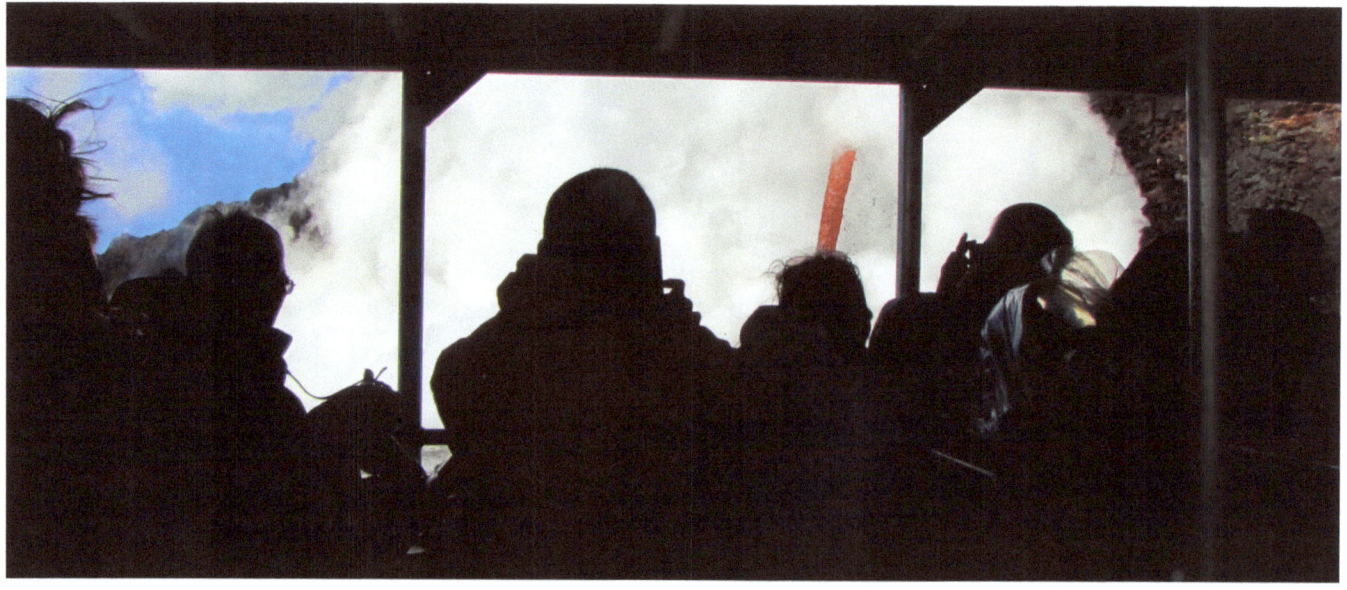

Getting up close to the Lava Spout   Kelly Hart

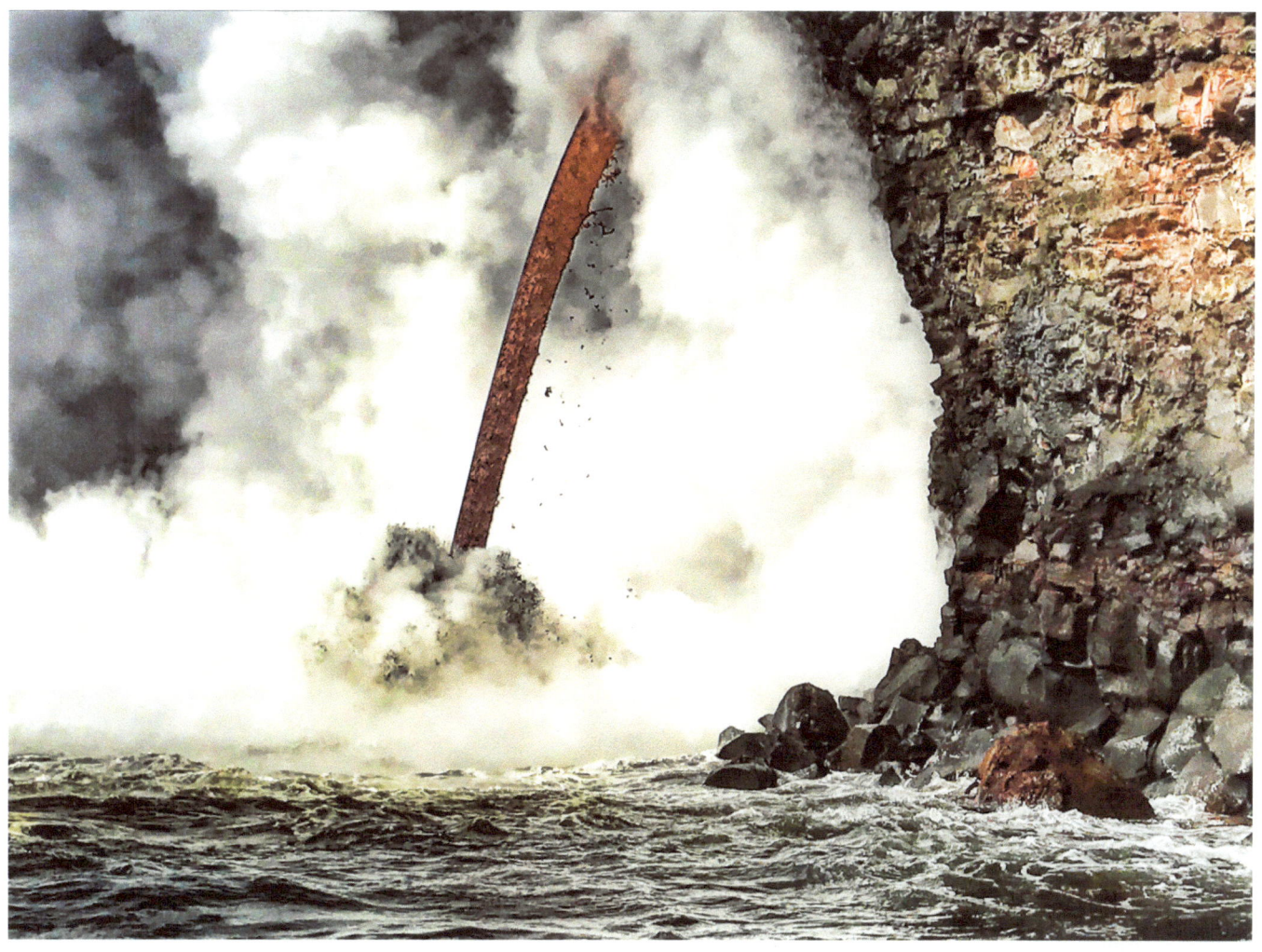

Artery

Molly Hart

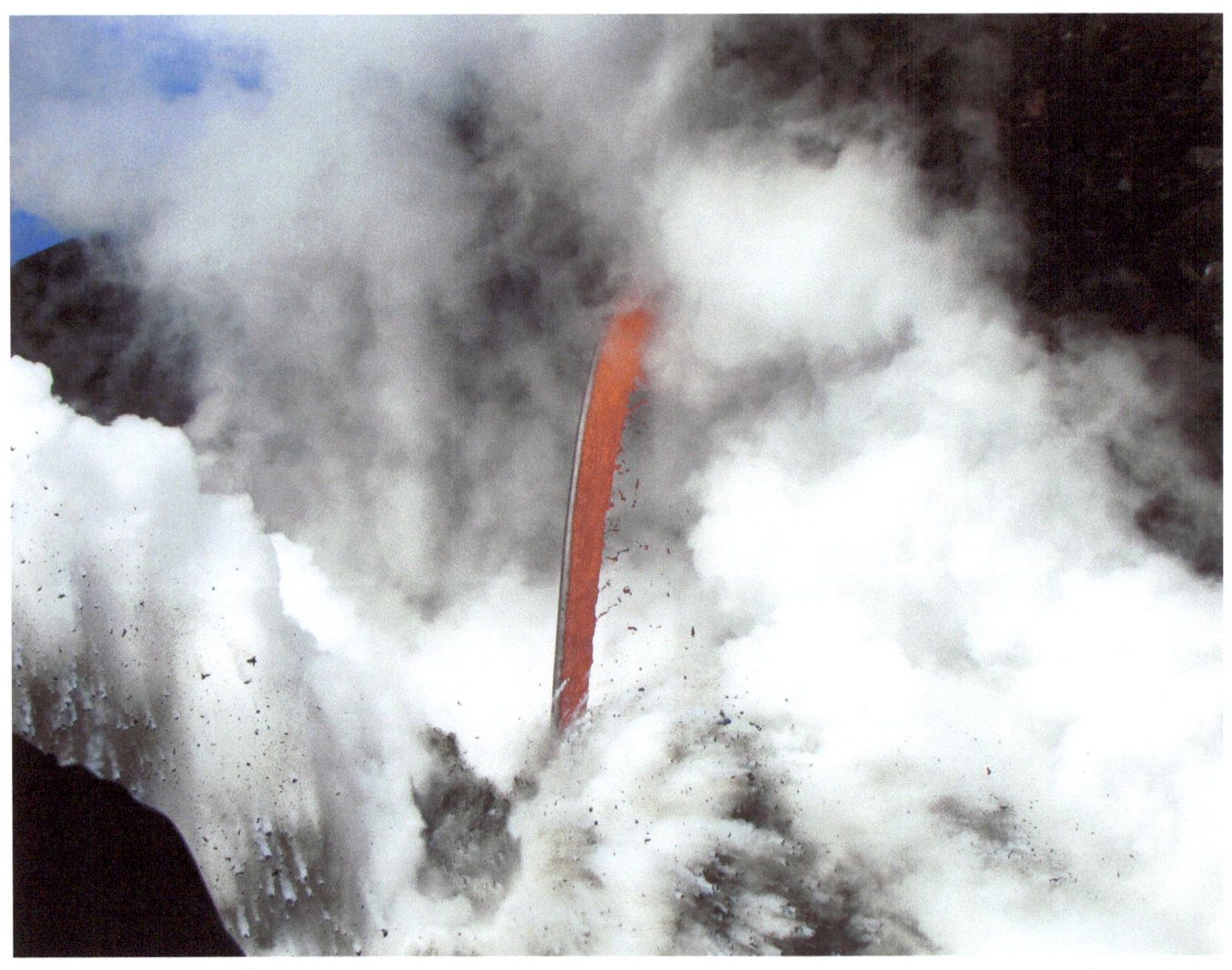

Blood of Mother Earth   Kelly Hart

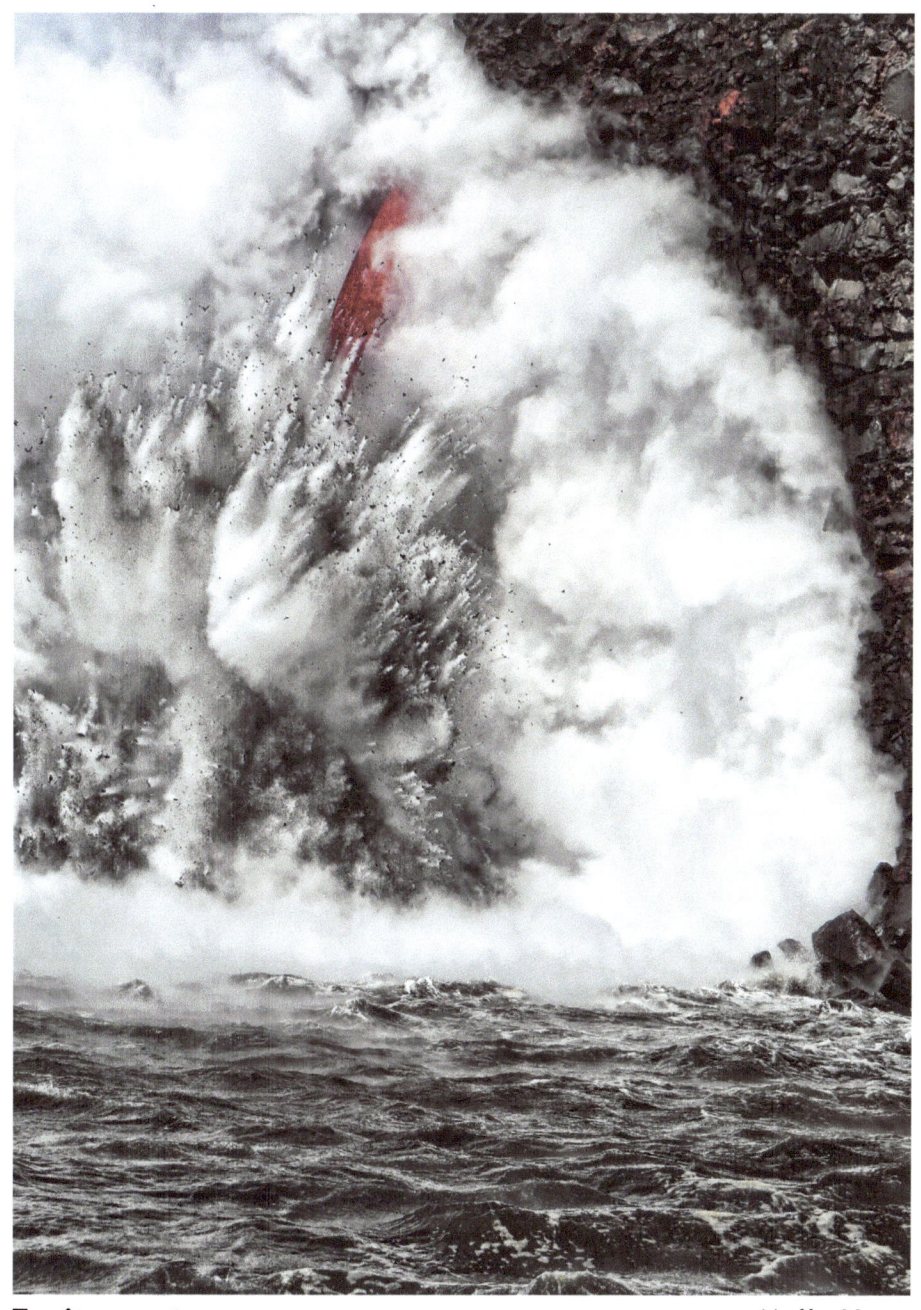

Excitement   Molly Hart

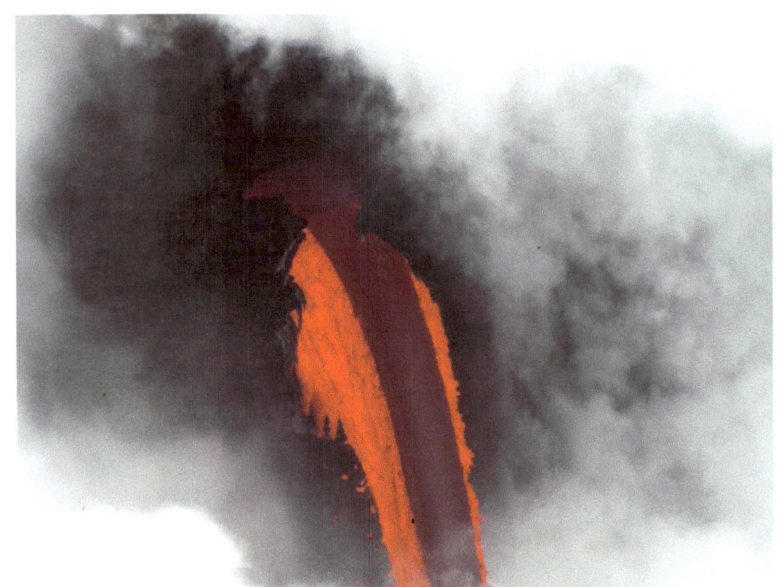

Orifice   Kelly Hart

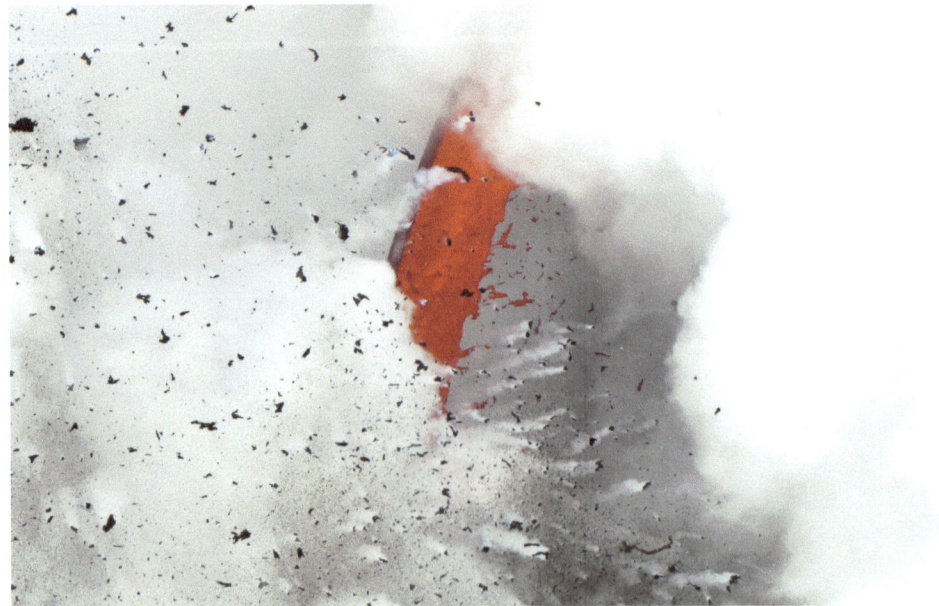

Blast   Kelly Hart

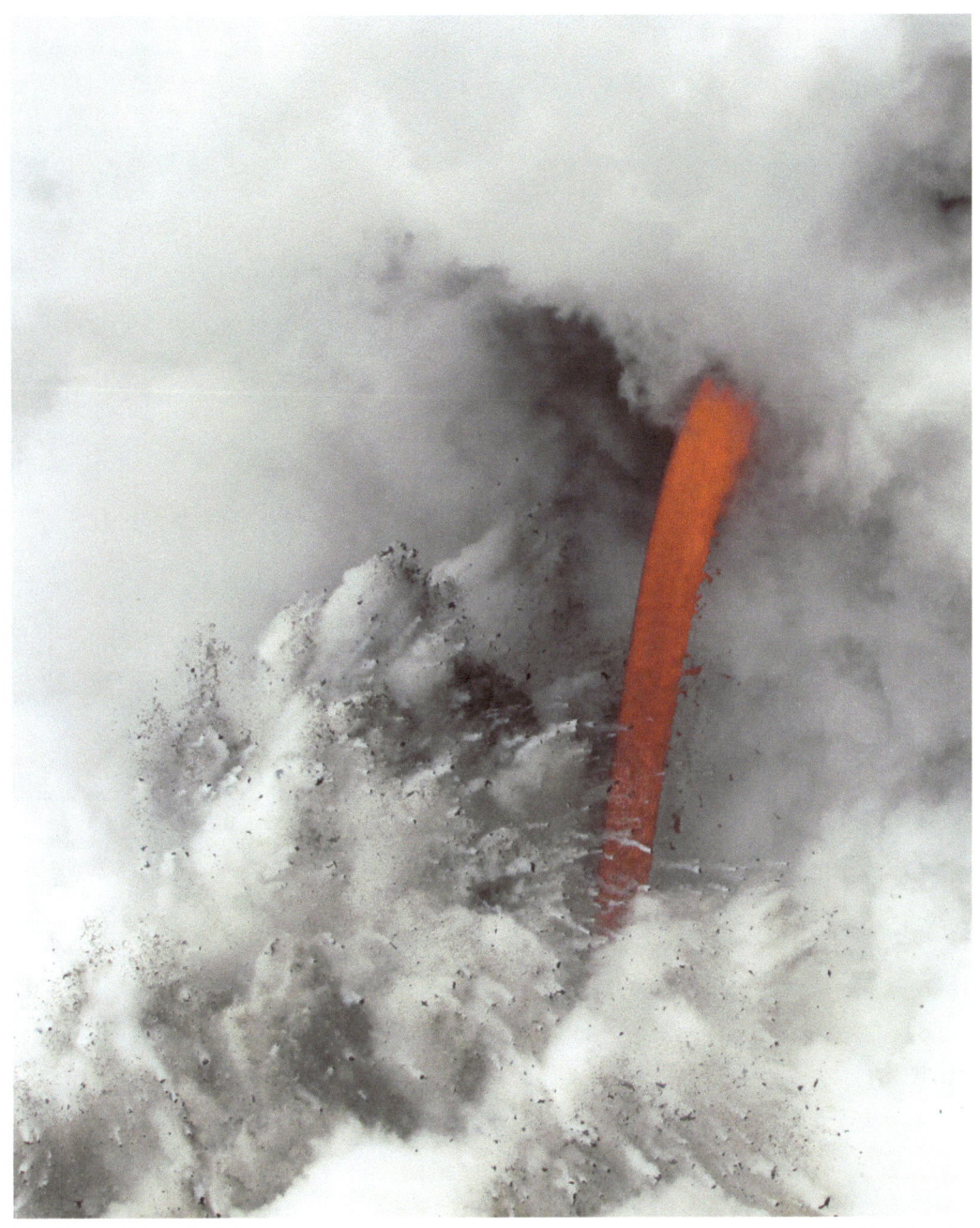

Hell and High Water   Kelly Hart

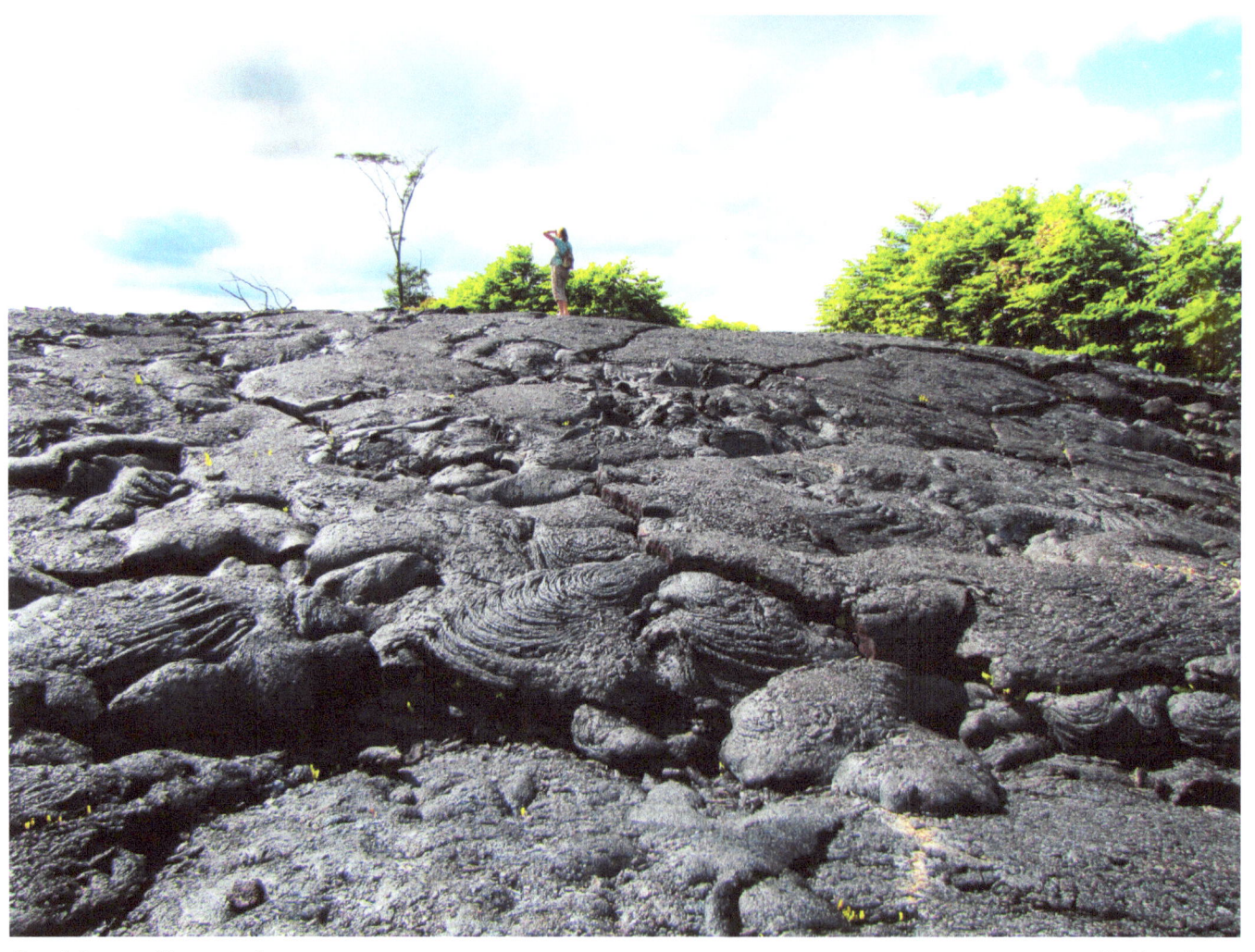

Cool Lava Mountain

Kelly Hart

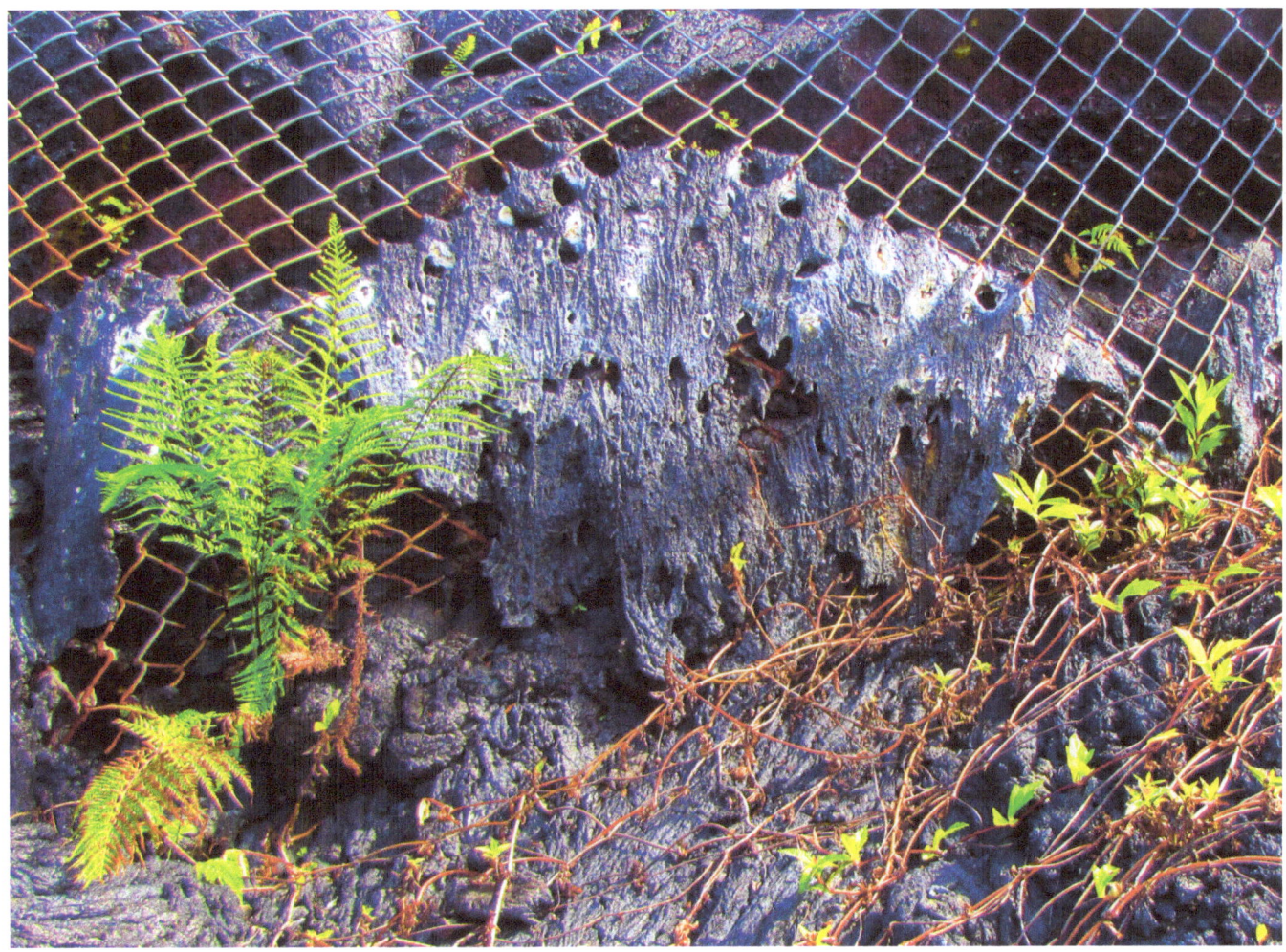

Don't Fence Me In   Kelly Hart

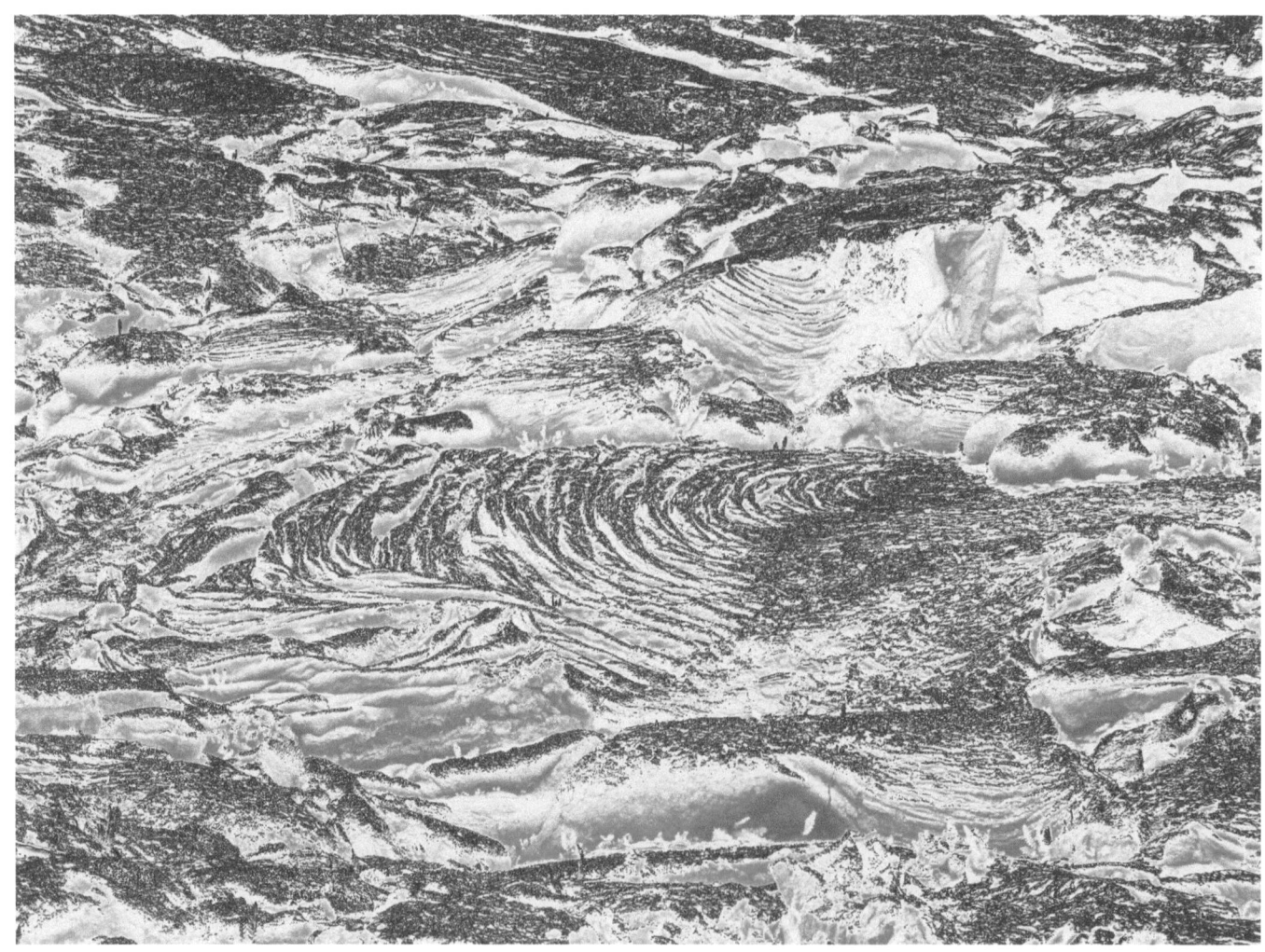

Puddles

Kelly Hart

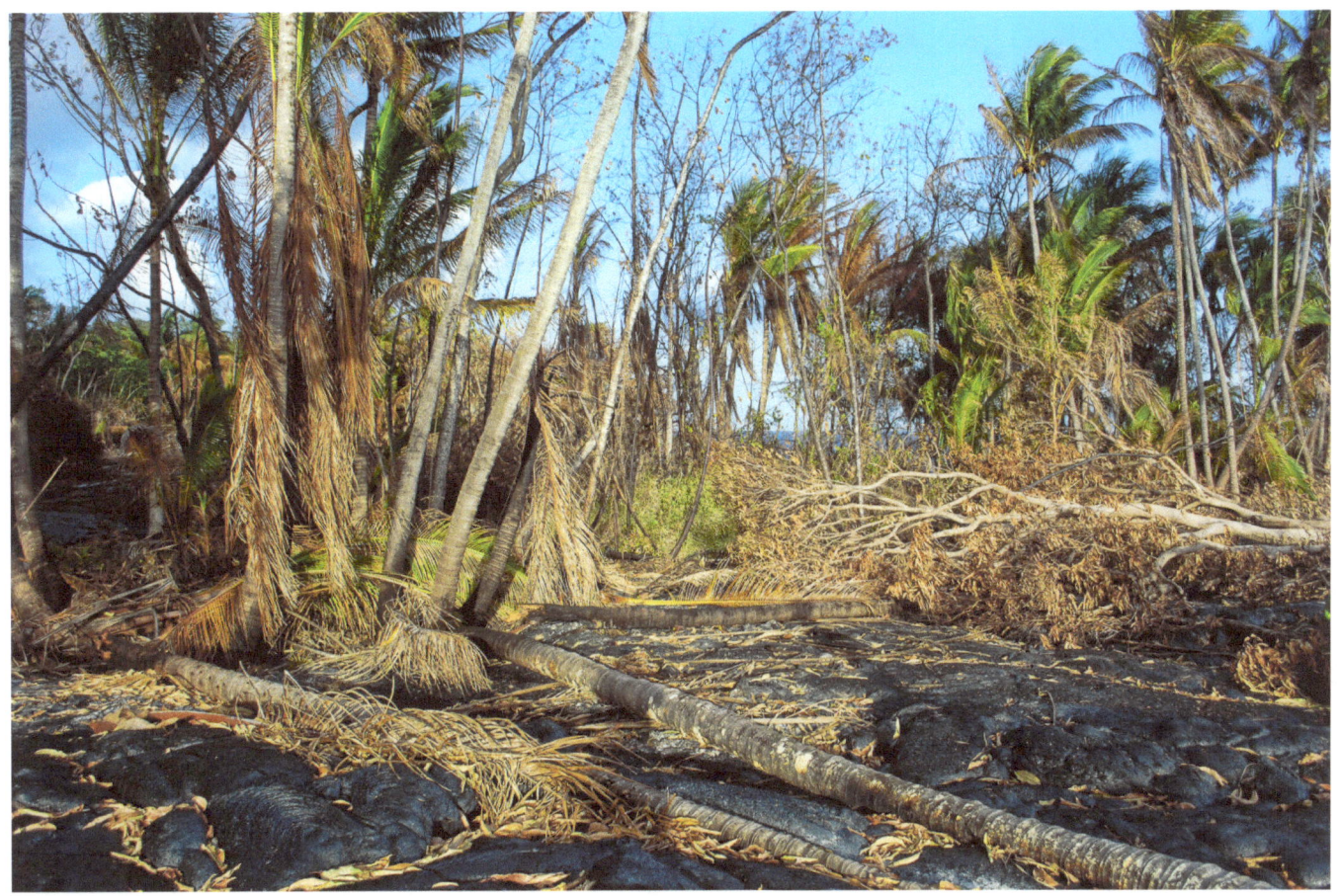

Lava Zone One

Molly Hart

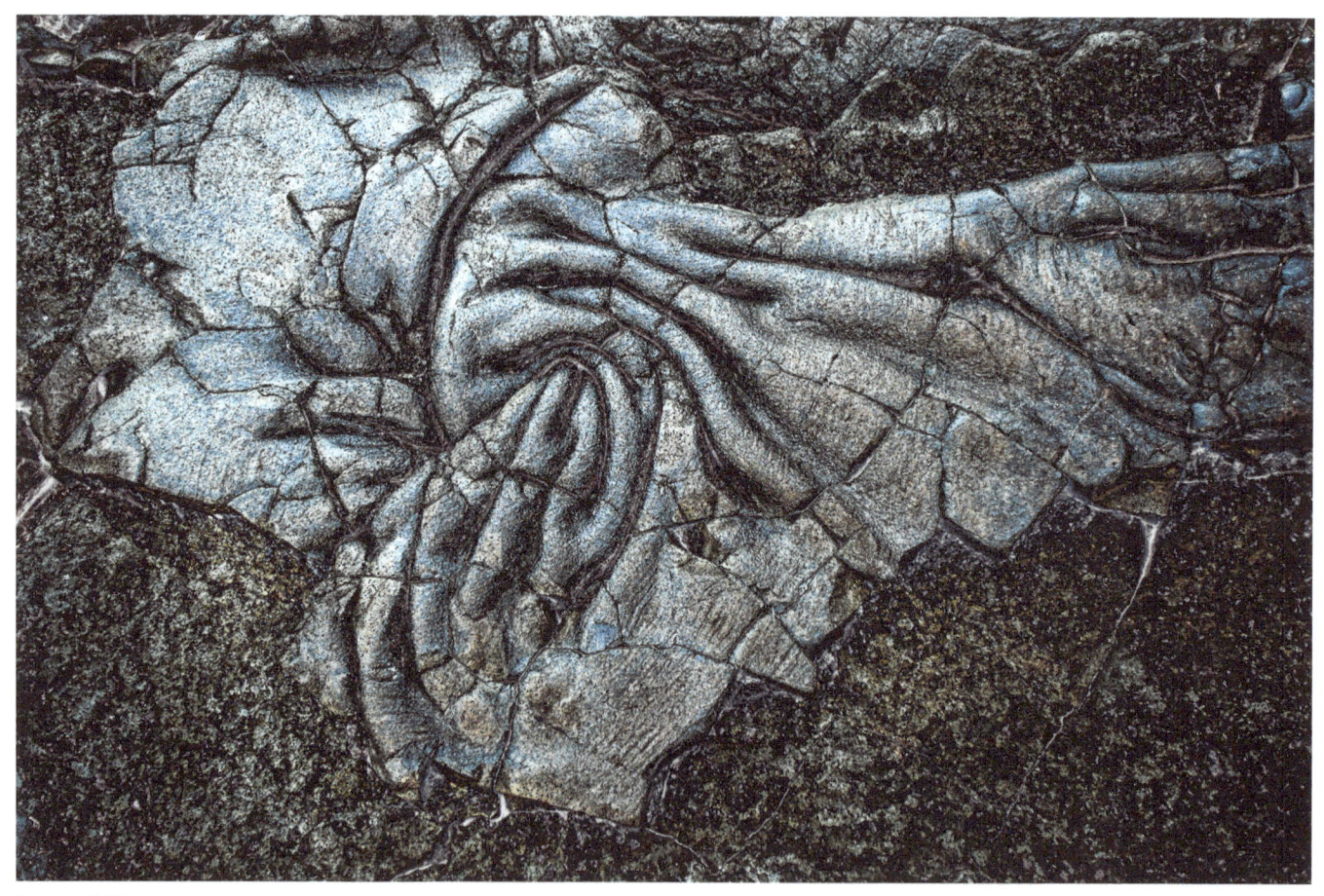

Lava Wings

Molly Hart

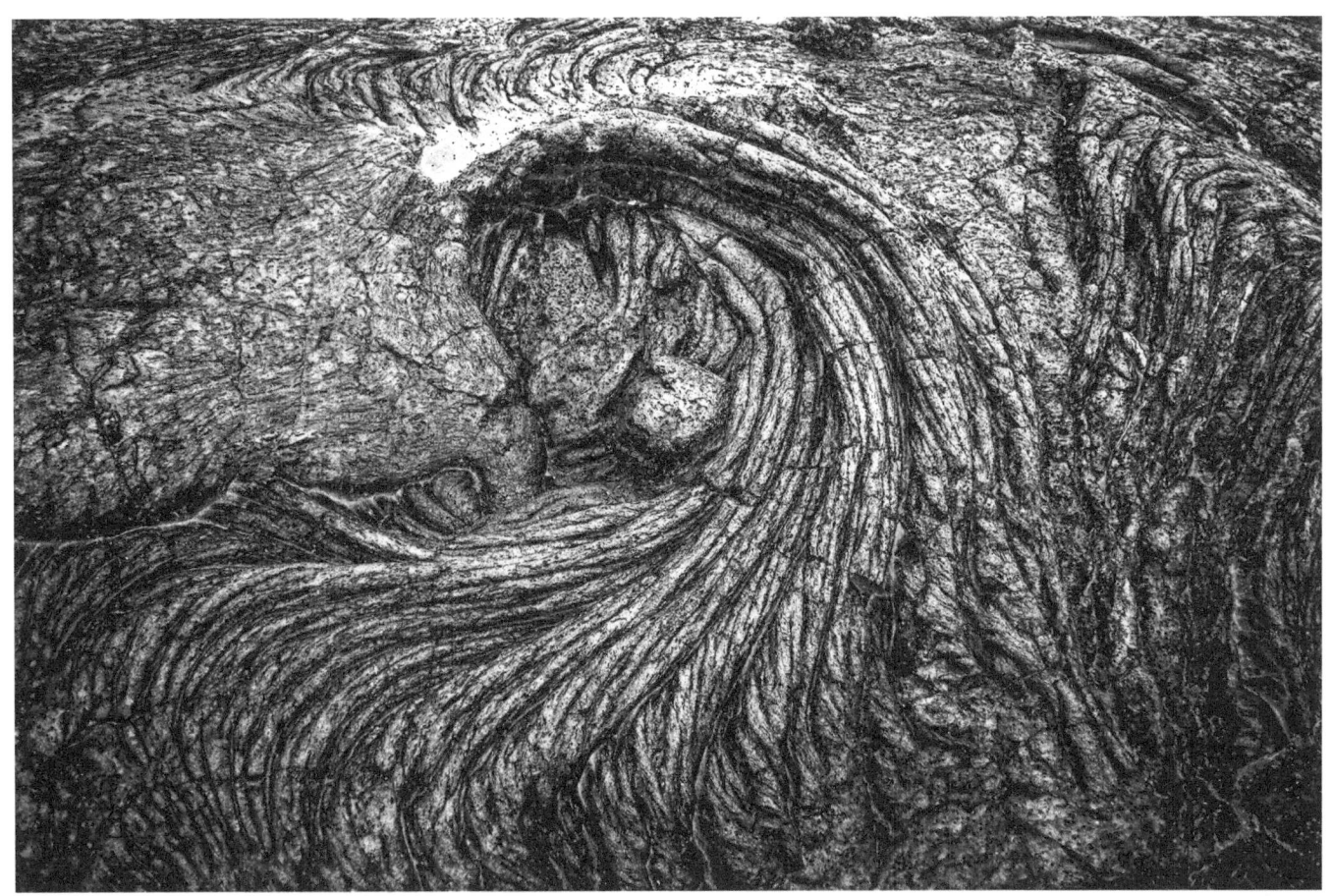

Frozen Wave   Molly Hart

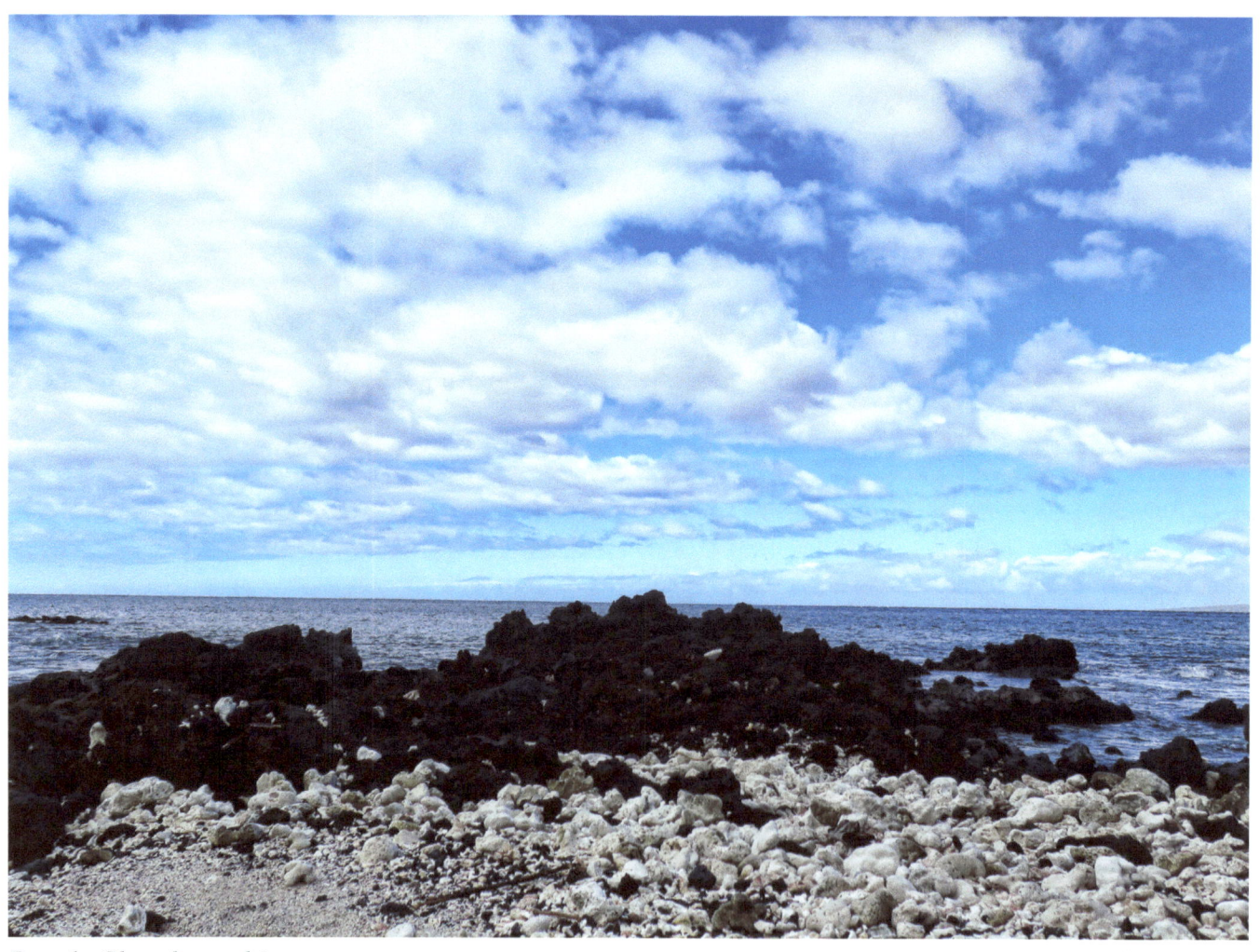

Coral, Clouds and Lava   Molly Hart

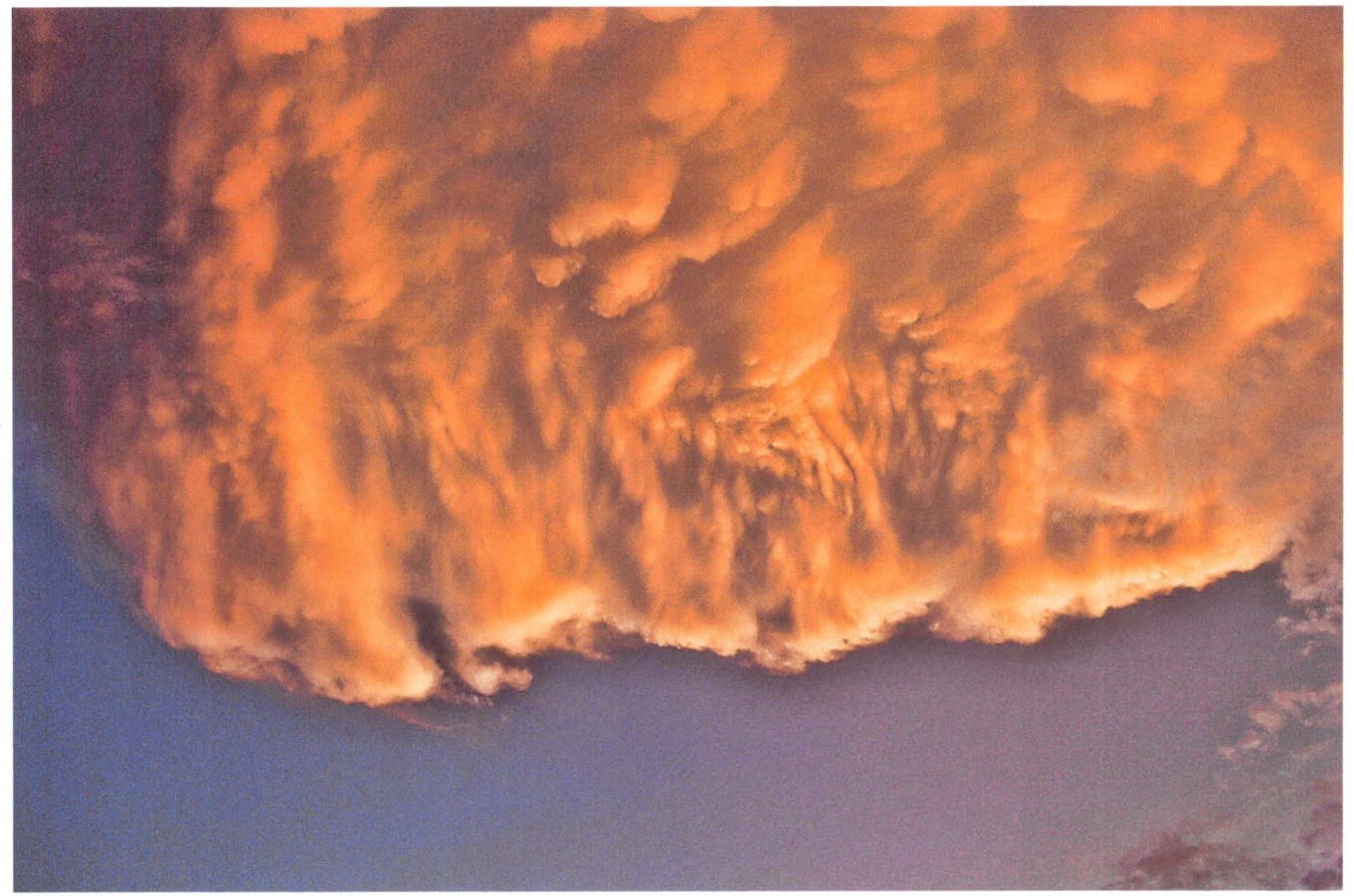

Day Surrenders

Molly Hart